A Long and Healthy Life

The Facts about High Level Wellness

Dr. Neecie Moore

Validation press

Published by Validation Press

All rights reserved. No part of this book may be reproduced in any form without written permission from the publisher. This book is intended to be a reference only. It is not intended to be used for diagnosis or treatment of disease. Before making changes in your diet, your medication, or your exercise program, consult with your physician.

Copyright © 1998 by Dr. Neecie Moore
Cover by Scott Hamilton
Book design and composition by Chris Roth
All images copyright www.arttoday.com. and Zedcor Desk Gallery

Printed in the United States of America
ISBN: 0-9660700-1-1

Other books by Dr. Neecie Moore:
The Missing Link:
    The Facts about Glyconutrients
Designing Your Life with Designer Foods:
    The Facts about Phytochemicals
The Miracle in Aloe Vera:
    The Facts about Polymannans
Bountiful Health Boundless Energy Brilliant Youth:
    The Facts about DHEA

First Edition
1 2 3 4 5 6 7 8 9 10

$12.95 Softcover

Contents

Dedication 5

Introduction 11

The Case for Nutritional Supplementation .. 23

The Case for Exercise 47

The Case for Recreation 83

The Case for Healthful Being, Eating and
    Loving 99

Bibliography for High Level Wellness 121

Index 135

Dedication

Over the past three years, my life has been transformed in an outstanding way. The journey began three years ago when I attended a seminar in Fort Worth, Texas, called "Unleash the Power Within." At that seminar, I saw thousands of college students, CEOs, moms, dads, young people, and senior citizens join hands and hearts to change their lives. At the end of the first evening, thousands of us broke through our fears and walked on fire. In the course of that evening, I had the marvelous privilege of meeting an extraordinary lady who would become a mentor to me in the following years.

The second leg of my journey occurred in Kona, Hawaii, in a seminar called "Financial Mastery." I met the same marvelous lady, and she once again touched my life in a dramatic way. I was nervous attending this seminar because I knew absolutely nothing about investing, the stock market, or advanced money matters. With her gentle spirit, she assured me that in her recent past she'd been in an identical position of ignorance and the same workshop had helped her overcome her fears and had launched her into absolute financial freedom. (No, I didn't walk on fire this time, but I climbed a 50-foot telephone pole and formed a commitment bridge with my buddy.)

The third leg of my journey occurred in Fiji. This incredible and awesome lady touched me in a way that was absolutely life-changing. This seminar, "Date with Destiny," occurred just as I was embarking on some major changes. My mentor sat with me and encouraged me as I changed my "life's questions," making new decisions about my values and beliefs. She imparted words of wisdom which were to shape my destiny over the next couple of years.

I saw this remarkable woman again in Denver, Colorado, where I served as staff at another "Unleash the Power Within." Her warmth, encouragement, and reinforcement took my new decisions to a deeper level.

The next several times I saw her, at "Trainer's Academy" and "Life Mastery," clarified what I so admired about her. She cheered us on as we walked on 40 feet of fire and climbed a 50-foot telephone pole, stood on top and leaped 15 feet to a trapeze.

She is a perfect picture of femininity clothed in strength and power. I realized that in running a foundation to support and empower prisoners, homeless persons, women and children in shelters, and many others, she remained soft in spirit, strong in courage, powerful in transforming lives. It is that character that I long to become. My thanks to you, my love to you, my admiration to you…

Becky Robbins.

Special Thanks to

My publisher, partner, and dear cousin, Brent Bouldin, who constantly aspires to high level wellness, providing the motivation for the creation of this book.

Chris Roth, our layout designer and artist, for serving up a superb work of art once again!

Scott Hamilton for another gorgeous cover design.

Rick Pribbernow, my booking agent, who works hard with a great big smile, and is the best dancer in the world!

All the wonderful people who make being on the road so much fun: Ray Robbins, Ferris Haddad, Karen Jenkins, Phyllis and Bob Hart, Gary Sanford, and so many others.

Acknowledgments

I am so very blessed to have a life full of people who are so wonderful. I could take this whole volume to mention them all. Thanks from the bottom of my heart to all my friends, family, and loved ones. I would like to acknowledge:

Red and Sissie Moore, my mother and dad, who are my greatest gifts and inspirations in my life;

Ruana Grace, my sister, and my dearest friend, whom I love, admire and cherish;

Kimberly (my right-hand woman) and Rodney Parker, Jason Jones, Paul (the funniest person I know), and Rebekah (the cutest cheerleader on earth!) Grace, my nieces and nephews who light up my life;

Andrea, Kelli, and Colleen Holt, my precious girls, who bring great love and laughter into my life (I love all of you dearly!);

Ben and Jack Watson, for being such terrific young men;

Seymon Olshansky, my dear friend who has taught me the real meaning of "God Bless America";

Shelby (my little doll) and Tyler Frasard, Zac Russell, and Austin Morris—the newest members of my family who make their grandparents so proud;

Jamille Maher— the oldest member of my family (almost) who makes every reunion a "whip cream gathering";

Diana Rivers, my long-time roommate and dear friend who keeps our hearts close;

Judy Moon, who taught me about running in another life long ago (I love you in our new life too!);

Rachael and Sarah Berry, the prettiest girls in Canada, for capturing my heart;

Kathy Hodges, for making Durango feel like "home";

Judy (a.k.a. "RWB or Bust!"), Ellen, Carolyn, Earlene, Patti, Roseanne, Dora, Suzette, and all my other Baton Rouge friends, who provide such love for my mother, the greatest gift they could give me;

Jeff and Barbie Ogg, who will always be part of my family and "that special friend" no matter how far away they are;

Dr. Sterling Sightler, M.D., for taking such great care of our family, for being a cutting edge physician, and for having a heart bigger than Texas (even if she *is* in Louisiana);

Mary Klaasen, Caroline Sime, and Susan Gwaltney, my study group, and all of my wonderful friends in the Joy Luck Investment Club, who provide great camaraderie as we make money together;

Dr. Howard Tobin, Dena Williams, Nina, Machelle, and Wondrea for taking such great care of me, helping me achieve my dreams and being such wonderful friends;

Philip Achemon and Candice Cobb for keeping my hair in great shape and providing a fun and exciting year as we awaited the arrival of Samantha Bryn ("Peanut");

My Fristers (Mary Ellen, Susan, Shari, Ginny and Anita) for being more than friends, and just like sisters;

And last, but not least, Gary Watson, who keeps me laughing, gives new meaning to the weather channel, and belongs on a John Deere tractor! ("What *could* I do?")

In Loving Memory of

Mary Scott, "Nanny," who took such excellent care of my girls in their younger years and kept us all laughing!

And

Bob Neeley, a man of great integrity, a philanthropist and dedicated friend. Bob and his wife, Kerry, were a beautiful picture of what love is meant to be. His best friends (TEAM-O!) Geoff Appold, Kerry, Jerry Shelton and Nick Voinis are a great testimony to the marvelous person that he was. His friends are a reflection of the various admirable aspects of Bob's personality. As played at his service and as sung beautifully by Celine Dion, "Our hearts will go on and on…"

Introduction

Taking care of our health and our bodies is one of the most honorable challenges that we can accept. Yet it's staggering how many of us fail to do so.

I vividly recall an incident in my preadolescence that I can only snicker about now. I was watching *The Johnny Carson Show* with my mom, and an "older lady" came on his set for an interview. I can see her now as if it were only last night when I saw the show. She was wearing nicely starched jeans, a plaid shirt; her hair was long and curly, and she bounced on the set with so much zest that I felt immediately connected to her. I distinctly remember thinking, "You know, if I could look and feel like her when I get old, I wouldn't mind getting old at all." I asked my mom how old she was, and my mom replied, "I think she's about 40." (My...how our perception of "old" changes over time!)

Several days later, we were watching the same show when another lady came on who looked old and decrepit. She had on a flowing dress with multi-colored flowers that looked like a muumuu. She walked on the set cautiously and slowly, almost limping. Johnny was interviewing her about a recent illness and her recovery. Throughout the interview, she puffed on a cigarette she had mounted in what appeared to be an ivory cigarette holder. I distinctly remember my thoughts as I watched: "I hope I never get that old." I asked my mom, "How old is she anyway?" My mom thought a minute and responded, "Oh, I think she's in her mid-30s."

At that young age, I made a commitment to myself to figure out how to take care of my body so that it would look like Johnny's first guest! And throughout my life, when I have needed to motivate myself with better self-care, I have booted up the picture of the second guest in my mind. It's all the motivation I've ever needed to get back on track!

Taking care of our health and our bodies is one of the most honorable challenges that we can accept. Yet it's staggering how many of us fail to do so.

The grim statistics regarding disease and health care costs are quite sobering. According to the *Monthly Vital Statistics Report* (June 1997) 2,322,265 people die annually in the United States. The report names the ten leading causes of death:

* Heart disease (733,834)
* Cancer (544,278)
* Stroke (160,431)
* Chronic Obstructive Pulmonary Disease (106,146)
* Accidents (93,874)
* Pneumonia/Influenza (82,579)
* Diabetes (61,559)
* HIV/AIDS (32,655)
* Suicide (30,862)
* Chronic Liver Disease/Cirrhosis (25,135)

Interestingly, many of these diseases could be prevented with healthful lifestyle changes (Moore, 1994, 1995, 1996, 1997).

Health care costs are difficult to comprehend. During 1996, national health expenditures exceeded $1 trillion dollars, and by 2002, they are projected to exceed $1.5 trillion (Thorpe, 1997). Think about that: A trillion is a one followed by twelve zeros (1,000,000,000,000). Even as we spend this much money on health care, incidence of illness and disease continues to increase.

I've devoted much of the past several years to the study of health and wellness. I have written and published four books on the topic of nutrition and health care: *Bountiful Health, Boundless Energy, Brilliant Youth: The Facts about DHEA* (1994), *The Miracle in Aloe Vera: The Facts about Polymannans* (1995), *Designing Your Life with Designer Foods: The Facts about Phytochemicals* (1996), *The Missing Link: The Facts about Glyconutrients* (1997).

In each of these books, I reported scientific research validating various natural methods of addressing illnesses from arthritis to viruses. I have also made a case for preventive practices, for the positive impact of nutritious eating on our long-term health, for the value of maintaining our health with nutritional substances, and for the absolute necessity for exercise.

My rigorous appearance schedule keeps me on the road before audiences frequently. I love addressing the audiences, answering their questions, and signing their books.

One evening after an appearance, I was sitting in a booth eating dinner with my publisher. I noticed I was particularly drained that evening and was musing over why I was so fatigued. My publisher remarked, "I don't find it so amazing: You lectured an hour, answered serious questions about illness and disease for an hour, then signed books for an hour while people queried you further about sickness."

After some thought, my response was: "You know, I want to continue to share my research results with people who are sick or whose loved ones are sick, but I want my next book to be about wellness. If I could lecture an hour on wellness, answer questions about staying well, and sign books while talking to people about how great they feel, I know I'd come away refreshed and invigorated instead of drained and exhausted."

This book is dedicated to those of you who—as I did as a preadolescent—believe that there are zestful, healthy ways of living that take the sting out of aging…to those of you who are absolutely committed to getting and staying well.

The challenge is that there are no shortcuts, no effortless "shake 'n bake" formulas, no "drive through" solutions, and no avoiding exercise and healthful eating!

I had a humorous client session a few years ago when a woman called in and had to see me immediately on an emergency basis. My assistant rearranged my schedule to accommodate her, and the client rushed in the door almost frantically at her appointed time.

Almost breathless, she flung herself into a chair and rushed right to the point: "I've got to look better and feel better. I have to. I'll do anything. I mean anything! But it's got to be quick. And I don't have time to do the gym thing. But I know you write those books about what to do, and I've got to do it." She handed me a spiral notebook and a pen and said, "Just write down what I have to do, and I'll do it."

I smiled, took the notebook, took a deep breath, and wrote these words on her page: "Slow down, love yourself, and call me when you have the time to do the 'gym thing.'" I took a deep breath in and slowly exhaled, then handed the notebook back to her.

I wasn't sure if she would storm out, tear up the note, or glaze over. Much to my delight, she laughed out loud, leaned back into her chair, threw up her hands and exclaimed, "I get it! I get it!" She did get it, and the last time I saw her, she looked and felt great.

High level wellness takes time. It takes commitment. It takes patience. I think it's a lot like my garden and my small stock portfolio. I didn't plant my daffodil bulbs one day and pull them up the next to see if they had roots growing. However, after months of maturing in the ground, being cared for quite gently, beautiful yellow flowers bloomed from lovely waxy green leaves.

Likewise, I didn't invest my money in stocks and expect to have a huge profit the next day. I knew it would take time. I knew there would be ups and downs in the markets—days when I would be thrilled I had invested, days when I thought I had made a huge mistake. However, I also knew that long term statistical data indicates that "stocks have out-performed all other investments for two hundred years" (Staton, 1998, p. 26). The research data marked my course for me; the rest was up to me.

So it is with our health care. The research data tells us what is necessary. The rest is up to us. Let's make one clear distinction: There is a difference between being free of disease and enjoying high level wellness. What is the difference? It's the difference between waking up in the morning and mumbling, "Oh God! It's morning again!" or waking up with a smile and proclaiming, "Thank God! It's morning again!" It's the difference between getting through each day or experiencing bountiful life each day. It's the difference between having tunnel vision and thinking that what you do today won't affect your health long-term; or knowing with absolute certainty that how you take care of yourself today will affect your long-term wellness for many years.

I invite you to accept the challenge to achieve high level wellness and zestful living. I've created this fifth book to I'll share with you both the research data and my personal regimen.

Once after returning from a visit to my Mamaw's house as a preschooler, my Sunday school teacher asked me if I had gone to church while visiting my grandmother. I told her that I had. She asked what my grandmother did at her church. I thought about that a moment. All I knew was that she *loved* her church, *believed* in her church, and *worked* hard at her church. I responded quite innocently, "I don't really know, but I think she's the head cheerleader."

Like my Mamaw, I *love* high-level wellness, I *believe* in zestful living, I *work* hard at it…and I'll be your head cheerleader as you take on the challenge.

Chapter 1

The Case for Nutritional Supplementation

> Commitment for life is an absolute must in your supplement program... commitment and patience.

Alternative and natural therapies are on the rise in North America! A study conducted in Minnesota found that two thirds of the households surveyed had used alternative health care (Freeman, 1997). Researchers found those results to be representative of the national statistics.

I loved the response of the people surveyed. The article abstract reported, "A most important aspect of such investigations is to improve the understanding of why patients choose these unconventional remedies. For many patients, the answer is simple. They believe these alternative treatments work" (Freeman, 1997).

The patients gave further feedback and reported that physicians represented "high tech" to them, and alternative practitioners represented "high touch."

The distinction between "high tech" and "high touch" can be easily evidenced by making a trip to your local hospital and watching the busy-ness of the doctors, nurses, and other staff as they rush through the ward, hooking up machines, writing case notes. Then visit your local health food store, or a meeting of one of the many groups that network-market health care products. There, you experience the sense of care and understanding, the feeling of "family."

A study reported in the *New England Journal of Medicine* indicated that there are about 425 million visits annually to alternative health care providers (Eisenberg et al., 1993). Visits to primary care physicians averaged about 388 million the same year. Expenditures for unconventional therapy were about $13.7 billion (even though three quarters of that was paid out of pocket) (Eisenberg et al., 1993).

A huge part of the alternative/holistic health care movement is the use of nutritional supplementation. Nutritional supplements are already a $6.5 billion-a-year industry, and the industry is continuing to grow at a rapid pace (O'Donnell, 1997).

A study revealing that about 46 percent of the population uses dietary supplements also describes the characteristics of those who take supplements most often (Slesinski et al., 1996). The study found that daily use of supplements was highest among

* Women
* Those 75 years of age and up
* Those with more than 12 years of education
* Former smokers
* Light or nondrinkers

Interestingly enough, the same study showed that the diets of those who take supplements tend to be lower in fat and higher in fiber than those of the general population.

Approximately 50 percent of athletes (Sobal and Marquart, 1994) and 50 percent of pharmacy students (Ranelli et al., 1993) use nutritional supplements.

Nutritional supplementation can no longer be shrugged off as "something that a few weird people do." As health care costs have risen, as disease has become more prevalent, and as quality of life has become more of an issue, people are looking to the health benefits of supplements.

My Beliefs about Nutritional Supplements

I believe nutritional supplements make a major difference in the quality of life. My four previous books have focused on the research demonstrating the impact of supplements on disease. However, I believe supplements have an even greater impact on wellness.

I have to admit that my interest in nutritional supplementation was sparked in the late 1970s when I was faced with what could have been a serious health challenge. However, I am in excellent health now, and I am more committed to taking the supplements I find helpful to me than ever before in my life!

Commitment for life is an absolute *must* in your supplement program…commitment and patience. Just as I don't plant my daffodil bulbs and expect to see yellow flowers the next day, I also don't take supplements and expect miracles the following day.

We have been inured to the pharmaceutical industry and its instant results. We take a pain pill for a migraine headache and watch the clock as the fifteen minutes crawl by until we expect relief. However, that relief also is sometimes accompanied by unwelcome side effects, including constipation, abdominal irritation, nausea.

Nutritional supplements may not offer immediate results; however, much of the time, the relief they do offer is without side effects. I love the new name that has emerged for supplements: nutraceuticals. Although I have not been able to determine who coined the term, it refers to foods which have medicinal properties. And certainly, most of the time these nutraceuticals have far fewer side effects than pharmaceuticals.

However, even when people discover the value of nutraceuticals, I am often amazed at the lack of commitment some have to their supplement program when all seems to be going well in their lives. For example, I met a woman about a year ago who suffered severe menopausal symptoms: night sweats, hot flashes, emotional swings, headaches. I reviewed research with her regarding supplements that might offer her relief. I suggested she take the material to her physician and develop a plan with him.

Three months later, a man approached me with absolute glee at one of my speaking engagements. He said, "I have to thank you for giving my wife back to me." He then explained who she was and the marvelous results she had experienced. I was delighted for both of them.

Last month, I attended a national rally for a nutraceutical company. The same woman approached me and explained that she just didn't seem to have any energy. I was actually surprised, because the same supplements that she had begun taking with her doctor's approval have also been shown in the literature to increase energy levels. I asked her how much she was taking. She said, "Oh, I got to feeling better, and I don't take those anymore."

I light-heartedly chided her, and insisted that she resume her supplement program *and* make the commitment to take them for life. She promised she would do so, and then laughed as she said, "You know, the only reason I'm willing to believe you about this is because you don't sell any of them!"

I encourage you to make the same commitment to your nutritional supplement program. Commit to it for life!

My Personal Nutritional Supplementation Plan

I am absolutely committed to my plan! So you might be wondering, "Well, what is yours?" I had always been hesitant to share my personal supplement program with my readers, because it is an individual thing. Not everyone has the same needs, the same goals, or the same health history.

However, I was in Chicago recently making a presentation at a health rally, and I mentioned my commitment to my program. A man from the audience asked what mine was. I hesitated just for a moment, then responded, "Okay, I'll tell you what it is. But be very careful. If you duplicate it, you will wake up in the morning looking just like me…5'7", long blonde hair, and you'll talk just like me too!" The audience laughed, because they got my point. Then I shared my regimen.

I will share it here again; however, you should not necessarily duplicate mine. I share it with you as my personal commitment that I will continue taking my supplements for life. I learned in my psychological training that making a public commitment requires more accountability and creates a greater likelihood of success. I take these supplements daily:

* Enada (NADH) 5 mg
* Plus (Wild Mexican Yam) 3 daily
* Ginkoba (Gingko biloba) 120 mg
* Phyto-Bears® (phytochemicals) 20 daily
* Man-Aloe® (stabilized *Aloe vera*) 3 daily
* Ambrotose® (glyconutrients with monosaccharides) 4 daily
* Shaklee Energizing Soy Protein Drink Mix (Soy protein with B vitamins) 3 T daily
* Firm (Wild Mexican Yam in transdermal form) applied abdominally twice daily
* Profile (daily vitamin supplement geared for my type)
* Citracal (Calcium Citrate) 1,500 mg daily
* Sport - 2 daily following a hard workout
* LifeSpan I™ (precursor to Growth Hormone) 2 daily

The second question that I am often asked is why I have selected the supplements that I take. Again, this is a personal decision which should not dictate your own supplement program, but there are specific reasons why I have selected the supplements I have selected.

Enada, Plus, Ginkoba

Unfortunately, there is high incidence of Alzheimer's disease in both my maternal and paternal family history. My mother's mother, Mamaw (whom I referred to in the introduction) died of Alzheimer's.

My mother is the youngest of six. The sister just older than she also died of Alzheimer's a few years ago.

My father's mother died of Alzheimer's many years ago. His younger sister died of this heartbreaking disease just a few years ago.

Recently, I interviewed a physician, and he took my family history. At the completion of the interview, he remarked, "Well, you sound like a good candidate for Alzheimer's." Amused by his insensitive comments, I replied with great confidence: "No, I'm not a good candidate for Alzheimer's, I'm a good candidate for Plus and Enada!" Plus, made with *Dioscorea villosa*, which is a precursor to pregnenolone and DHEA (Dean and Morgenthaler, 1991; Leblhuber et al., 1993; Roberts, 1990) and Enada, or NADH Nicotinamide Adenine Dinucleotide, (Birkmayer et al., 1993; Birkmayer et al., 1997)—a cousin to the B vitamins—have been shown to be preventive of Alzheimer's disease, and to offer symptomatic relief.

Dioscorea villosa

I take Ginkoba for similar reasons. Several studies have shown *Ginkgo biloba* to be effective in treating memory loss in patients with dementia (Allain et al., 1993; Grassel, 1992; Itil and Martorano, 1995), as well as being effective in sharpening focus and mental processing (Warot et al., 1991). With my demanding schedule, I have a pressing need to be focused and to be able to concentrate despite many distractions. I also have a heavy calendar of personal appearances that keeps me traveling nationwide. As I speak to groups, I meet many people I see again at national health rallies. Being able to remember names and faces is very important to me, and many find it surprising a year later when I can remember their name and/or their story. I truly believe that this supplement helps me in this endeavor!

Ginkgo biloba

Phyto-Bears®

When I speak to audiences, I ask for a show of hands for the number of people who take Phyto-Bears® and the number of people who take Phyt-Aloe®. Then I tease them, asking why on earth anyone would swallow a capsule when they could eat a gummi-bear? I've only had one answer that I think makes sense. One lady told me that the Phyto-Bears® stuck to her dentures! Otherwise, these delightful little bears are filled with the same phytochemicals (in lesser amounts) as the Phyt-Aloe®...and they are quite delicious!

I wrote an entire book about the benefits of various phytochemicals found in fruits and vegetables (Moore, 1996). I eat far more servings of fruits and veggies than are recommended by the United States Department of Agriculture (1992). They recommend three to five servings of veggies daily, and two to four of fruit. Although my fruit and vegetable consumption far exceeds this amount, I know that phytochemicals are only available in vine-ripened, recently picked produce. I know that most of the produce in supermarkets meets neither of these criteria, and I'm not willing to risk a deficit of these phytochemicals.

I am particularly interested in the ability of the phytochemicals to prevent various cancers. I lost my dear Aunt Mamie to cancer several years ago, and my mother is now a seven-year survivor of ovarian cancer. I am determined to keep my body cancer-free, and I believe the phytochemicals in this product are a great aid in realizing my objective!

Man-Aloe® and Ambrotose®

Man-Aloe® is a product that is basically stabilized *Aloe vera*, along with other monosaccharides in a base of soy lecithin. I wrote an entire book about the "miracles" of *Aloe vera* (Moore, 1995). I take this supplement because I believe it keeps my immune system strong and keeps me in great health! I also believe in the power of soy to act as a natural estrogen in my body. (See more details below where I discuss Energizing Soy Protein Drink Mix.)

I take Ambrotose® for very similar reasons. This product contains all of the glyconutrients necessary to enhance intercellular communication in the body! My book, *The Missing Link: The Facts about Glyconutrients* (Moore, 1997) explains the importance of the glyconutrients in detail. I take these supplements because I know they keep my immune system strong, ward off depression (which I struggled with at one time in my life, but no longer have time for!), and prevent autoimmune disease.

Shaklee's Energizing Soy Protein Drink Mix

I use Shaklee's Energizing Soy Protein Drink Mix to ensure that my body has adequate protein. I simply put it in the blender with fruit and fruit juice and prepare my "power shake" daily. Research has shown the heavy consumption of soy in Southeast Asian populations to be associated with reduced incidence of cancer and cardiovascular disease (Barnes, 1998). Research has also shown soy protein to be preventive of osteoporosis (Ishida et al., 1998).

Soy itself is believed to have these preventive properties because the isoflavones, or phytoestrogens, are very similar to the estrogens we produce (Anthony et al., 1996). However, many women seeking hormone replacement therapy due to menopause or hysterectomy are concerned that some of the female cancers are believed to be hormone-dependent (Adlercreutz, 1995). Happily, phytoestrogens found in soy can provide the benefits of estrogen while actually *preventing* breast cancer (Herman et al., 1995; Stephens, November 1997; Horn-Ross, 1995).

In addition to these marvelous benefits, phytoestrogens found in soy have also been shown to be powerful antioxidants (Ruiz-Larrea et al., 1997) and preventors of prostate cancer (Stephens, August 1997) and colon cancer (Brandi, 1997).

Since I am post-hysterectomy and also have a family history of female cancers, I have refused traditional hormone replacement therapy. Still, I remain concerned about my high risk factors for osteoporosis and heart disease. I feel certain that the phytoestrogens in soy address both of these issues. And I can assure you that I am symptom-free of any estrogen deficiencies (from hot flashes to depression)!

Firm

I also believe some of the same phytoestrogen benefits are available in Firm, a lotion in a base of wild Mexican yam and glyconutrients. Although it was developed as a thigh cream, its greatest benefits lie in the transdermal application of this precursor to pregnenolone and DHEA.

In past seminars I've asked: "How many of you suffer with PMS?" However, I stopped asking the question because I typically had more males than females raise their hands! I'm sure many men who have lived with females combating PMS think they have suffered worse than their partners have. Still, I can assure you that living in a body with PMS is no fun!

Dioscorea villosa

The transdermal application of these pre-hormones can be effective in relieving the symptoms of PMS (Kamen, 1993).

Profile

I take Profile, a daily vitamin supplement. The product comes in three different versions to fit a person's exact nutritional needs. Readers who have access to the Internet can complete a 50-question survey and learn immediately the specific formula best for their specific body type. Simply go online and type in this address: **http://web1.mannatech-inc.com/profiling.cfm.** There is no charge for the survey or its results.

LifeSpan I™

I use LifeSpan I™, which is a natural precursor for growth hormone. I use this product because research has shown that growth hormone reduces body fat, increases lean muscle mass when combined with exercise, and increases energy (Solimini, 1996). In one specific study, men were administered growth hormone for a period of six months (Lawren, 1990). At the conclusion of the study, their lean body mass had increased nine percent, and they had realized a fat loss of 15 percent. These results equated to erasing 10 to 20 years from their respective biological ages. Additionally, growth hormone has been shown to strengthen the immune system, sharpen the memory, improve sexual function, provide better quality of sleep, improve mood, and lower blood pressure and cholesterol (Klatz and Kahn, 1997).

Citracal

Citracal, a calcium citrate supplement, is an important part of my supplementation. It became critically important several years ago when I seemed to be on a mission to break every bone in my body! I managed to traverse my entire childhood with no broken bones: I climbed trees, rode bikes without holding the handle bars, jumped out of swings, played on jungle gyms, rode skateboards, jumped on pogo sticks, and walked on high stilts.

At age 39, shortly after my hysterectomy, I was having the time of my life on a trail ride. My "brother" Glen and my "sister" Pat were in their bright red wagon, being pulled by their two gorgeous mules. There were about a hundred of us on horseback and in wagons on a beautiful country road in east Texas. I had just left the group to visit with a friend whose home we passed. My friend showed me the most beautiful newborn kittens you have ever seen. After holding my pick of the litter for awhile, I realized I needed to catch up with the group. I nudged my horse, Cassidy, and we were off. I got in line at the back, waiting for the tree line to widen so that I could make my way back to Pat and Glen's wagon.

The kids in the wagon in front of me threw an ice chest out the back of their wagon, spooking Cassidy. Up in the air Cassidy reared. I instinctively grabbed the reins to hold on. Pulling him back kept him up in the air until he finally stepped backwards into a ditch and fell over on me.

Thank God, the only injury I sustained was a break in my left leg. I thought it was "one of those things," and I healed very quickly.

A year later, while playing baseball with my daughter, Andrea, on the beach in Galveston, I was running for a ball when I stepped in the moat of a sandcastle. I tripped and fell, catching myself with my right arm. I heard a snap, but little did I know what had really happened.

Later, as we were cooking burgers on the grill, I thought for sure I had simply dislocated my arm. While Andrea stayed out to bring in the burgers, I went in to get the buns and trimmings ready. By the time my daughter came in, my arm hurt so badly I could hardly breathe. I tried to eat a hamburger, but after a bite or two, I couldn't tolerate the pain any longer.

I went to UTMB (The University of Texas Medical Branch) Emergency Room. Before I could finish signing in, the nurse took one look at my arm and rushed me straight back to surgery.

The bone was not simply broken; it was shattered in dozens of pieces.

At a health rally following this accident, I signed hundreds of books with my left hand while my right arm was resting in its bright purple cast. (This time I had Man-Aloe®, and I believe that my quick recovery can definitely be attributed to it!)

This incident caused me to wonder if I could be suffering from bone loss or the beginning of osteoporosis. But I think I had the common lackadaisical attitude: "That can't happen to me!"

However, a few months later I slipped and fell in Colorado—not a hard fall at all. The result was a tibia plateau fracture. By now I was certain that I needed to pay attention to my calcium intake. However, I was focused on figuring out how to do life on crutches. (I was nonweight bearing for 12 weeks, meaning my foot didn't touch the ground that entire time!) What a challenge it was! Had it not been for my assistant,

Kay Jackson, and my niece, Kimberly Parker, I don't know how I would have made it through that ordeal. After months of physical therapy, I was on my feet again!

And I forgot about the need for calcium supplementation.

Then several months later I was preparing to go visit my mentor, Dr. Patricia Love, in Austin, Texas. Walking into the airport terminal, I was hit by a moving vehicle. The result was another tibia plateau fracture, along with three other breaks in my leg, a torn lateral collateral, and a severed ACL (accruciate ligament).

I thought that all the king's horses and all the king's men could never put me back together again. However, my wonderful surgeon, Dr. Robert Scheinberg, and my dedicated physical therapist, Dale Smith, worked expertly and patiently with me over the next year. The doctors who read my MRIs and x-rays couldn't say if I would be able to walk again, but in record time I was running, skiing, horseback riding, and dancing! Once again, I think the wonderful line of supplements that I take shortened my recovery time. Everyone (except God and me) was surprised by my recovery rate!

After this incident, I didn't neglect my need for calcium. I have supplemented with it faithfully ever since, and I have had no further injuries, thank God!

According to the National Institutes of Health (1994), calcium intake is essential in the following doses:

> Birth to six months – 400 mg/day
> Six months to twelve months – 600 mg/day
> Ages 1 to 5 – 800 mg/day
> Ages 6 to 10 – 1,200 mg/day
> Ages 11 to 24 – 1,500 mg/day
> Ages 25 to 50 (Women) – 1,000 mg/day
> Pregnant or Lactating Women – 1,500 mg/day
> Postmenopausal Women on ERT (estrogen replacement therapy) – 1,000 mg/day
> Postmenopausal Women not on ERT – 1,500 mg/day
> Ages 25-65 (Men) – 1,000 mg/day
> Ages 66 and above (Men and Women) – 1,500 mg/day

According to a survey reported by *Tufts University Health and Nutrition Letter* (1997), most adults consume only about half of the total calcium they need in their diets. The diet is the optimal source of calcium. In fact, diets high in calcium from food indicate lesser occurrence of kidney stones. However, if one must take a supplement, calcium citrate taken on an empty stomach is best absorbed (Jibrin, 1997).

After reviewing the research, I found Citracal to be what I felt my body needed to regain strong bones. "Clinical trials conducted among postmenopausal women show that the administration...of Citracal increased bone density, prevented fractures of the spine, and preserved body height" (*Harvard Women's Health Watch,* 1996; Zerwekh et al., 1997).

I also use apple juice or orange juice fortified with calcium citrate in my "power shakes." Research has shown both of these juices carry highly absorbable calcium when in citrate form (Andon et al., 1996).

Sport

Following a hard workout, I also take two Sport capsules. This product has a wild Mexican yam base, and also contains herbal extracts that aid the body in recovery following physical exertion. I find that I have no soreness in my muscles when I use these capsules.

The Challenge

I find that most people spend more time researching the next vehicle they intend to purchase than they do researching and studying what their bodies need for optimal health!

I encourage you to do your own research based on your health concerns, your family's medical history, and your personal health goals. When you discover what you need in regard to nutritional supplementation, I encourage you to make a lifetime commitment.

Isn't good health an investment far greater than any you could put in your savings account? After all, without your high level wellness, you couldn't enjoy that money in your account, no matter how large the amount!

Take a moment right now to write your commitment to your supplementation program:

_____

_____

_____

_____

_____

_____

Chapter 2

The Case for Exercise

> The benefits of exercise are enormous. In fact, I believe exercise is the foundation of high level wellness.

In order to achieve high level wellness, you've got to get movin'! There are no shortcuts, no excuses, and no alternatives!

One of my mentors, Anthony Robbins, says that if you have enough compelling reasons why you are determined to do something, you will succeed. Take exercise, for example: If you know why you must exercise—to avoid disease and achieve high level wellness—your success is certain if you take these things to heart.

My goal is to give you compelling evidence that will motivate you to make new decisions, change old beliefs about exercise, and get movin'!

I understand the sentiment: "Oh God! Let's not talk about exercise!" I owned that sentiment myself at one time. However, I began running and aerobic dancing back in the early 1980s, and I felt absolutely fabulous! Although I never totally quit, I slacked off during the years of graduate school. (I completed my last two years of undergraduate school in one year, completed my master's degree in one year, and completed my doctoral degree in two and a half years. Time was limited.)

Then I had a new excuse, a practice to build. I was working on staff at my church, working at a Christian School as a counselor, working at a nonprofit counseling agency, and building my own practice. Where was the time to exercise?

And the excuses went on until, reading one evening, I found a quote that steered me back in the right directions:

> Take control of your physical health so that you not only look good, but you *feel* good and know that you're *in control* of your life, in a body that radiates vitality and allows you to accomplish your outcome (Robbins, 1991, 27).

I got up from that reading session and looked in the mirror. Although I was still exercising sporadically,

I saw a tired young woman, slouched with fatigue, a bit flabby, and living a life that ran me instead of me running my life.

That was a transforming moment for me. I absolutely determined at that moment to change my life so that I looked and felt great and radiated vitality. Today, I believe I do. And I wish you the same ability to look *and feel* great!

So let's leverage you with the "why's!"

The Facts about Americans and Exercise

The facts are plain, simple and disheartening. According to the first-ever Surgeon General's Report on Physical Activity and Health, 60 percent of Americans don't get enough exercise daily to stay healthy and 25 percent aren't exercising at all (Squires, 1996). Among adolescents aged 12 to 21, about 50 percent do not exercise. Enrollment in high school physical education classes dropped from 42 percent in 1991 to 25 percent in 1995 (Centers for Disease Control, July 1996). Additional findings in this astonishing study indicated that men exercise more than women; white adults exercise more than African Americans or Hispanic adults; and more affluent people exercise more than less affluent people (Centers for Disease Control, July 1996).

Our inactivity as a nation is evident! People wait in line or drive around for ten minutes to get a parking space close to the front door of the grocery store or shopping mall, even when the weather outside is gorgeous! Riding mowers can be seen clipping the lawn at houses on very small lots. Moving sidewalks in airports are jammed full of passengers standing still while being transported to the next gate. Walking has been prohibited on many golf courses where golf carts now reign. Escalators have replaced stairs in many public areas. And then there's the remote control....

What is the result? We are an overweight country. I was in an airport waiting for a delayed flight to depart in Salt Lake City, Utah, just last week. I had already used my layover time to do aerobic walking through the airport for an hour. Instead of "awfulizing" the delayed flight and working myself into a stressed frenzy, I decided to conduct some informal research in preparation to write this chapter.

I walked up to the main corridor connecting all the concourses in the airport. I sat down and made three columns on a piece of paper. I headed the columns as follows: 1) Normal weight; 2) Overweight; 3) Seriously overweight. I decided that overweight would be assigned to anyone who appeared to be 30 to 50 pounds overweight. Seriously overweight would be assigned to anyone who appeared to be more than 50 pounds overweight and seemed to be huffing and puffing, red-faced, as they struggled to move through the airport.

The results were interesting. I had time to observe almost 400 passengers before my flight was called. Three were actually following my regimen and were obviously using their layover time to walk aerobically through the airport. The "normal weight" column received 38 marks, the "overweight" column received 192 marks, and the "seriously overweight" column received 133 marks.

The next time you are caught waiting somewhere, design your own little study and become aware of the weight condition of our society. I can assure you that such observation will inspire you!

The Facts about Exercise in Other Countries

Our Canadian friends struggle with obesity just as we do. A survey examining the health habits of

Canadians (The Canadian National Obesity Survey), revealed that 51 percent of Canadians are overweight. In addition, 96 percent of Canadians said they believed exercise had an effect on weight loss, but only half of that same group had ever attempted to use exercise as a weight loss measure. Thirty-nine percent of Canadians reported exercising less than twice weekly (*Canadian News Wire,* 1997).

Our friends in Australia have improved their exercise performance. A study conducted between 1989 and 1990 revealed that 41 percent of men and 49 percent of women were walking for exercise. The 1995 National Nutrition Survey indicated that 53 percent of women and 59 percent of men were walking for exercise. When the focus broadens to include all forms of exercise, 64 percent of men and 67 percent of women exercise regularly (Bennett, 1995).

In Switzerland, 58 percent of adolescent boys are physically active as are 46 percent of adolescent females. Thirty to 40 percent of the young adults get enough exercise for prevention of disease. However, 70 percent of adults between 55 and 74 get sufficient exercise (Lifestyles, 1998).

These were the most impressive results in my review. Congratulations to the Swiss!

In both Scotland and England, a Sports Council and Health Education Council survey revealed that the activity levels of about 70 percent of adult men and women were below the level considered to promote good health (WHO Regional Office for Europe, 1998).

Why We MUST Exercise

The benefits of exercise are enormous. In fact, I believe exercise is the foundation of high level wellness. Dr. Robert Butler, founding director of the National Institute on Aging, said it quite well: "If doctors could prescribe exercise in pill form, it would be the single most widely prescribed drug in the world"! (Nelson and Wernick, 1998, 41).

Osteoporosis

Exercise can actually reduce bone loss in osteoporosis. The dangers of osteoporosis are often overshadowed by the concerns for cancer. However, more women die annually from fractures related to osteoporosis than from the combination of breast cancer, uterine cancer and ovarian cancer (Nelson and Wernick, 1998).

In Chapter One, I recounted my own up-close and very personal experience with falls and breaks. To my surprise, I found that over 240,000 people aged 50 and over experience hip fractures, (the most dangerous type), annually (Cummings et al., 1990). Of course, the majority of these breaks are related to osteoporosis. Half of those with hip fractures either die or can no longer live independently (Scott, 1990).

If you would like to avoid being among those sad numbers, here's good news: Exercise has been shown to be an excellent preventive of osteoporotic bone loss (Kano, 1998; Nelson et al., 1994). You may think this section is only for "old folks." However, studies have shown that even young people have significantly greater bone density and less body fat when they exercise regularly (Cullinin and Caldwell, 1998). One study examined college-aged young women. The study's dramatic results demonstrated that—even at that early age—bone density is significantly greater in an active group (Madsen et al., 1998).

Follow my lead on this one! If you want to avoid fractures and develop strong bones, get movin'!

My latest bone density report shows that I have the bone structure of someone ten years younger than my biological age!

Balance

As we reach midlife, our ability to balance declines. However, research has shown that exercise can improve balance (Shumway-Cook et al., 1997). Another study conducted by Nelson et al. (1994) observed two groups of women for one year. One group exercised regularly; the other group was sedentary. At the end of the year, the sedentary group scored 8.5 percent lower on a balance test. The group that exercised scored 14 percent better on the balance test than they had the previous year.

These results should encourage us to exercise to maintain our balance! I don't know about you, but I don't want to be stumbling around as I age. I plan to be line dancing when I'm 95, and if you've ever line danced, you know you must have excellent balance!

Cardiovascular Disease

Exercise can have a powerful effect on your heart. Many people don't realize that the heart is a muscle. When we lose weight in the absence of exercise, we often lose more muscle than fat. People frequently tell me: "I don't care what I lose as long as I lose it." They make such remarks because they aren't taking into account that their heart is also a muscle. The primary method of building the heart into a strong, healthy muscle is through aerobic exercise. Exercise has many positive benefits on our cardiovascular system.

Exercise has been shown to reduce blood pressure. One study examined the blood pressure rates of hypertensive patients following a 12-week aerobic exercise program (Arida et al., 1996). The participants realized a significant reduction in the diastolic blood pressure after the 12-week program. Another project conducted by the Department of Psychology at Syracuse University (Ewart et al., 1998) examined the effects of aerobic exercise on adolescent girls at high risk for blood pressure problems. These 88 young ladies were divided into two groups. One group took standard physical education classes; the other group took aerobic exercise classes. At the conclusion of the study, the girls who took the aerobic classes saw significant decreases in their systolic blood pressure. The two studies above support a mild aerobic exercise program as a powerful antihypertensive!

Cholesterol levels are another area of concern for those who want a healthy cardiovascular system. Once again: Exercise to the rescue! Because I am a runner and I have high HDL cholesterol (a level of 50 as assessed in my lab work one month ago) and low LDL cholesterol (53), I was quite interested in the results of a study regarding cholesterol and women runners. The study involved 1,837 female runners and found that their HDL levels increased with the increased numbers of kilometers these women ran (Williams, 1996). The results were the same, regardless of the diet!

Another study found that men aged 30 to 65 years showed lower LDL levels and higher HDL levels following 16 weeks of stationary bike riding for 30 minutes a week, and 16 weeks of 30-minute riding three times weekly (Iyawe et al., 1996). These are low levels of exercise that result in some pretty good changes in cholesterol levels, changes that are sure to produce a healthier heart!

Your heart should already be jumping up and down with glee at this moment…but there is more!

Cerebrovascular disease is common in older women. However, this disease can be prevented by regular aerobic exercise as a young woman (Hata et al., 1998). A study conducted in Australia indicated that aerobic exercise for 45 minutes four times weekly reduces all cardiovascular risk factors (Nolte et al., 1997).

Exercise also serves as a powerful rehabilitation measure for patients with coronary artery disease (Lavie and Milani, 1996). One hundred thirteen males with coronary artery disease were monitored for six years. The remarkable results indicated a significant retardation of the disease in patients who exercised moderately for approximately four hours weekly (Niebauer et al., 1997).

The heart is a muscle that we literally cannot live without. If for no other reason, we should exercise as a great gift to our heart! Dr Miriam Nelson (1998), Associate Chief of the Human Physiology Laboratory at Tufts University, sums it up well:

> When your cardiovascular fitness improves, you have more energy; you don't find yourself gasping for breath if you have to move quickly. Activities that stopped being enjoyable because they were such a struggle become fun again.

Diabetes

As I travel around the country appearing at health rallies, I am astonished by the number of diabetics who tell me that their health care provider has never encouraged them to exercise!

Exercise has been shown to prevent the development of non-insulin dependent diabetes, and it has also been shown to maintain the preventive effect for three months after the cessation of exercise (Shima et al., 1996). Patients who have this type of diabetes and who exercise experience improved insulin sensitivity and lower glucose levels (Wallberg-Henriksson et al., 1998). Both aerobic and resistance training have been shown to be effective with non-insulin-dependent diabetics (Eriksson et al., 1997).

The benefits of exercise for patients with insulin-dependent (Type I) diabetes have been proved as well. Exercise also increases insulin sensitivity and reduces blood glucose levels in patients with this type of diabetes (Fahey et al., 1996). A study involving adolescents with type I diabetes found that a combination of aerobic and resistance training (aerobic circuit exercise) effectively regulated glucose (Mosher et al., 1998).

About 12 percent of pregnant women experience gestational diabetes, a type of diabetes that occurs during pregnancy. Exercise has been shown to act as a preventive and stabilizer in this type of diabetes as well (Bung and Artal, 1996).

Diabetics should check with their health care provider before making any change to their self-care regimen. However, I certainly hope that your physician is up to speed on the latest research and recommends this nontoxic remedy—good old-fashioned exercise!

Depression

Early in my graduate career, I began focusing my studies on depression. Although I think my initial interest was an effort to heal my own bouts with the condition, I very quickly realized that the incidence of depression was much greater than I had ever imagined.

Over 17 million Americans struggle with depression annually (*Medical and Other News*, 1996). Another 10 to 12 million suffer from anxiety or stress reactions

(Penn State, 1998). Approximately 25 percent of women will experience depression this year (McFarling, 1997), while only six percent of men will do so (*Women's Health*, 1998).

The difference in the incidence of depression between genders is cause for speculation. Some researchers believe that the percentages are actually very similar between genders, but that men are less likely to acknowledge, report, or talk about depression.

However, there are physiological reasons why women are more prone to depression. High estrogen levels in women are believed to set the stage for depression by causing the secretion of cortisol. High levels of cortisol have been associated with increased depression. In addition, serotonin (a neurotransmitter produced in the brain) has been strongly correlated with freedom from depression. Women are less able to synthesize serotonin, setting the stage for higher levels of depression (*Women's Health*, 1998).

Depression still carries a social stigma, so many people forego seeking help of any kind. Researchers believe that only 25 percent of people with depression seek help (McFarling, 1997). Many people who are willing to step past the social stigma and acknowledge their depression are unable to get help because of the lack of insurance coverage for treatment. One study investigated 2,325 companies with over 100 employees. Researchers found that 43 percent of the policies had mental health coverage with more restrictive limits than medical coverage. Sixty-six percent had more restrictive cost coverage for mental health care than for medical services (Nicolosi, 1997).

When depressed people do seek help, the cost is often enormous. "The total cost of the disorder has been estimated at $44 billion" (*Harvard Mental Health Letter*, 1994). Unfortunately, even when patients do get help, two thirds have a relapse within five years (Painter, 1996). All I can say is that exercise is practically free (if you have a comfortable pair of shoes to walk in) and is effective in the treatment of depression. And  there are no relapses—unless your commitment to exercise lapses!

Many kinds of exercise have been shown to be effective in treating depression, but walking is particularly popular. "Exercise is important in the treatment of depression. Walking is best because it's distracting, physically challenging, offers an immediate sense of accomplishment, is non-threatening, and it's social" (McFarling, 1997).

Exactly how exercise works to alleviate depression is not totally clear. Scientists believe that secretion of endorphins increases during exercise. "Endorphin" derives from the same root word as "morphine," suggesting a reduction in the pain and suffering caused by depression.

> Depressed people suffer more than those with most chronic physical illnesses. Among serious illnesses, only advanced coronary artery disease results in more days spent in bed, and only arthritis causes more chronic pain. In the long run the social cost of depression is in the same range as the cost of AIDS, cancer, or heart disease" (*Harvard Mental Health Letter,* 1994).

Exercise can relieve the pain and suffering of depression. One study used 47 volunteers with physical disabilities to determine the effect of exercise on depression. After 12 weeks of aerobic exercise, the volunteers realized a significant decrease in depressive symptoms (Coyle and Santiago, 1995).

The School of Public Health at the University of California at Berkeley has been studying 6,000 adults since 1965. The ongoing study reveals a strong association between physical exercise and relief from depression (Exercise as Therapy, 1998). A study conducted at LaTrobe University in Australia demonstrated that Tai Chi, a gentle, non-strenuous, dance-type exercise program, produced students who were less depressed, anxious and tense and who enjoyed improved mental health (Jin, 1989). Scientists worked with 401 adults in Illinois and found that "exercise is associated with decreased symptoms of depression (feelings that life is not worthwhile, low in spirits, etc.), anxiety (restlessness, tension, etc.), and malaise (rundown feeling, trouble sleeping, etc.)" (Ross and Hayes, 1988, 770).

Depression and low self-esteem often accompany one another (*Washingtonian*, 1994). Once depression erodes a person's self-esteem, she feels unworthy of help or too helpless or void of energy to take effective action. When folks in this condition come into my office, I love to break this cycle. I ask them to name some of their favorite music. I go to my musical library and pull one of their selections. Then I put it on, turn the volume up, and invite them to dance. If they are not dancers, we just walk in time with the rhythm of the music. Just a three-minute song can break the pattern, and then the client can continue from there.

Exercise literally breaks the spiraling cycle of low self-esteem. A project in Minnesota showed that exercise was successful in reducing tension and increasing self-esteem in women in just two exercise sessions (Pronk, et al., 1995). At the University of Illinois, a 20-week exercise program significantly improved the self-esteem of participants (McAuley et al., 1997).

Research has clearly demonstrated exercise to be just as effective as other relaxation techniques in reducing stress: People who exercise have been shown to succumb to stress less than sedentary persons (*Consumer Reports on Health,* 1995). If you are depressed or stressed out, the answer is to get movin'!

Someone I love very dearly told me once, "I don't have a life—I have a schedule: I work; I'm the taxi service for my kids; I'm the maid for everyone at home." I simply responded, "Then pencil in a little time for the maid, even *she* gets time off!"

You can start with just a little exercise. Just park in the back of the parking lot at the grocery store; take the stairs at work; walk around the room while you're talking on the phone. You will feel so much better that I bet you will take your walking shoes to work and use half your lunch hour to walk at a neighboring mall. Get started. Start small and notice how much better you feel! The better you feel, the more you will want to exercise!

When I feel "emotionally challenged," I go for a walk and repeat my power words: "COURAGE! FAITH! COMPASSION! DETERMINATION!" This approach never fails! Within a matter of minutes, I go from "emotionally challenged" to "emotionally charged!"

Arthritis

Not too long ago, physicians advised arthritic patients to stop all forms of exercise, thinking vigorous activity might exacerbate their condition. Now medicine has come full circle, and we are acutely aware of the benefits of exercise for people suffering with arthritis.

We now know that exercise can induce changes in immune function, including a decrease in the CD4+ count. These results are helpful in regulating inflammation (Shephard and Shek, 1997), and they hold true even in cases of rheumatoid arthritis.

In the Netherlands, scientists examined the effects of exercise and sedentary behavior on 100 patients diagnosed with rheumatoid arthritis. After a 12-week exercise course, test participants experienced increased aerobic capacity, muscle strength, and joint mobility. In addition, there was no deterioration in the arthritic condition during this exercise period. After 12 weeks of sedentary behavior, all gains disappeared (van den Ende et al., 1996).

Some arthritic patients believe that they are too fatigued to exercise. Monitored 12-week exercise programs have demonstrated that exercise lessens fatigue levels while increasing strength and decreasing pain. In addition patients studied in this review were able to walk at a faster rate following the exercise program (Neuberger et al., 1997). Clearly, if you have arthritis, you will feel much better if you exercise! Exercise reduces pain while increasing muscle strength. (Noreau et al., 1995; Ytterberg et al., 1994).

Cancer

Exercise is a great preventive of cancer! Exercise produces antioxidants which destroy free radicals believed to cause cancer.

Running has been shown to be a powerful preventive of both lung and liver cancer

(Duncan et al., 1997). Prostate cancer is the most frequently diagnosed cancer in men. Exercise has been found to be a preventive of this cancer as well (Oliveria and Lee, 1997).

In Washington State, 537 patients aged 50 to 64 years old who were diagnosed with breast cancer were compared to women of the same age who were cancer-free. Scientists documented a reduced risk factor for the group of middle-aged women who exercised (McTiernan et al., 1996).

For individuals diagnosed with breast cancer, exercise can be very beneficial. Exercise has been shown to improve depressive and anxiety symptoms, while lifting self-esteem following breast cancer surgery (Segar et al., 1998). During radiation therapy associated with breast cancer, exercise has been shown to manage fatigue and improve physical functioning (Mock et al., 1997).

A review of the literature on various cancers reveals that exercise reduces fatigue, body fat levels and nausea, as well as improving psychological well-being (Dimeo et al., 1998; Friendenreich and Courneya, 1996; Schwartz, 1998). Colorectal cancer survivors who do not reinitiate their exercise program following surgery or treatment have a lower quality of life than those who do resume exercise (Courneya and Friedenreich, 1997).

Addictions

Exercise has proved effective in the recovery process of addicts. Exercise programs have a twofold effect on alcoholics in inpatient treatment. Those in the exercise program had less craving for alcohol than those patients receiving psychotherapy only. In addition, the exercisers reported feeling an internalized locus of control, a very important factor in successfully prolonged abstinence from alcohol (Ermalinski et al., 1997).

Food addicts have also benefited from exercise. In a study targeting binge eaters, 81.4 percent of those treated with an exercise program freed themselves of the practice. In addition, their depressive symptoms subsided (Levine et al., 1996). Exercise could be a powerful treatment for people struggling with eating disorders.

Exercise is excellent for you! Now you have the "why's", so why not get started?

My Personal Regimen

I am a dyed-in-the-wool exercise advocate! I will do most anything to get my exercise in! If my schedule demands it, I will get up at 5:00 a.m. to do my workout. And let me assure you—that is truly dedication: I have a nightshirt that expresses my sentiments about morning quite well. The shirt features a picture of a ragged Garfield, looking pretty grouchy. The caption reads: "I don't do mornings!"

I believe in a mixture of cardiovascular (aerobic) exercise and strength (or resistance) training. I am not interested in looking like a Charlene Atlas, so I use lighter weights at higher repetitions.

Wear a Heart Monitor

One word of caution before I give you my cardiovascular regimen. I don't think anyone should engage in cardiovascular exercise without wearing a heart monitor. To do so is like driving a car without a speedometer down an expressway well monitored by highway patrolmen. If you drive too slowly, you will be run over. If you drive too fast, you will get a ticket. (Don't you just love it when those lights start whirling in your rear-view mirror?)

A heart monitor tells you exactly the rate at which your heart is beating. Determining the optimal range is very beneficial for maximizing exercise benefits. The ideal range is referred to as your "target heart range" and falls between 60 and 80 percent of the maximum number of beats that your heart can pound out per minute. The simplest way to determine these numbers is to subtract your age from 220. The result is your heart's maximum rate. Now multiply that number by .60, and you will get the lower number of your target heart range. Multiply the difference between your age and 220 by .80, and you will get the higher number of your target heart range.

Here's an example:

I am 43 years old as I write this chapter.

220	177	177
- 43	x .60	x .80
177	106.2	141.6

Therefore, when I exercise, I try to keep my heart rate between 106.2 and 141.6. Personally, I prefer to warm up at the lower range, (about 110) for five to ten minutes; then I do my main workout at the higher range, between 135 and 142. Finally, I cool down for five to ten minutes at the lower range.

Now figure out your target heart range.

```
   220              ___ "A"        ___ "A"
-  ___ (Your age)   x .60          x .80
   _____ ("A")     _____ ("B")   _____ ("C")
```

Your target heart range is _____ (Put the number from "B" here) to _____ (Put the number from "C" here).

Now how on earth will you be able to keep your heart within those limits if you aren't wearing a heart monitor to tell you where you are at all times?

I describe the device for readers who've never seen one: The sensor itself mounts to your chest and is held in place by an elastic band. On your wrist, a watch-like apparatus provides a readout of your heart rate throughout your exercise.

These monitors were once quite expensive. Happily, the prices have become more reasonable in recent years. Straightforward models can now be purchased for as little as $79. They are a *must* for exercising within your heart range!

My Cardiovascular Workout

When I am home (which is rare these days), I do cross training. Cross training simply refers to doing a variety of aerobic exercises. I exercise for one hour three days a week, and 45 minutes three days a week (on the days when I add resistance training). On days when I exercise for one hour, I do ten minutes on each of six different pieces of cardiovascular equipment: a treadmill, a stationary bike, an elliptical walker, a stair stepper, and a skiing trainer that goes side to side (not a cross country ski machine).

When I am not at home, I run, rollerblade or cross train on equipment at a local gym. I think cross training is very important, because evidence suggests that the body becomes used to exercise when you do the same thing repetitively, and the exercise becomes less effective, especially for women (Waterhouse, 1993).

Yes, there is a difference between men and women in exercise. Let me give you a short biochemistry lesson to hone in on the differences. Lipogenic enzymes are the enzymes that carry fat into the cells. To clarify this analogy, we can equate lipogenic enzymes to water in a swimming pool. Unfortunately, women have more lipogenic enzymes than men, meaning that we carry more fat into our cells. To use the swimming pool analogy, we have more water to put into the swimming pool.

Lipolytic enzymes are those enzymes that carry fat out of our cells and into our system as energy. Let's equate those enzymes to the pump that carries water out of the pool. You guessed it—men have more lipolytic enzymes than women do. To return to our analogy, a woman's swimming pool would have a lot of water going into it and a small pump that didn't take the water out. Her pool would be full of fresh, cool water. (Pretty inviting in the kind of heat we have during Texas summers!) A man would have only a small amount of water going in, and a pump carrying a lot out, so his pool would be almost dry.

Now a cool, refreshing pool sounds pretty good! But when it comes to fat...that's not so cool, right? So what's a woman to do?

Exercise is one of the ways to decrease lipogenic enzymes and increase lipolytic enzymes.

Women often reach plateaus because these lipogenic enzymes have decreased, the lipolytic enzymes have increased, and the levels have settled at a new place with regular exercise as part of your program. However, when you cross train and keep your body guessing, the balance is upset: The lipogenic enzymes continue to decrease, and the lipolytic enzymes continue to increase.

Another way to keep these enzymes moving in the direction that we want them to move is by adding resistance (or strength) training.

My Strength Training Regimen

My goal is *strength* training, not gaining bulk in my muscles. I simply want to strengthen them and tone them so that I am a lean, mean fat-burning machine!

I learned a tremendous amount from Larry North (1997). He eradicated my disdain for weight lifting and encouraged me to start my program. His theory is that form is more important than how much weight you lift. Further, I love his philosophy: "No pain is gain. Less is more. The big lie in physical fitness has been the idea that you have to grunt to get fit, that you have to pant to get lean…I enforce a rule for 200 personal trainers I've hired. If they make any of their clients sore in the first two weeks, they'll be asked to leave" (page 78).

I've lost count of the number of gyms I had joined over the years. Although I enjoyed the cardiovascular exercise at all of them, I often tried to do a weight training program. The same thing happened in each incident. I would set up an appointment, and someone would weigh me, measure me, and then show me my workout on a variety of machines and with a variety of dumbbells. The following day, I would be in such pain I could hardly get out of bed.

For three days, I would be miserable, unable to imagine why anyone would do such a thing to his or her body.

After studying Larry North's work, I tried one more time. Actually, Larry's published advice and the encouragement of my daughter Andrea got me started. She said to me, "Ma, I want us to really work at toning up. Let's join the gym together and really work at it." I agreed (although there is nothing about her gorgeous body that needs to be toned up)! This time, I only lifted a bit more than was comfortable, and did small numbers of reps. Because I wasn't sore, I was willing to try another workout. Before I knew it, I was just as committed to my strength training as I was to my cardiovascular exercise.

I now do strength training three days a week. Because I am only toning, I do it on Monday, Wednesday and Friday when my schedule allows. If adjustments are necessary, I can shift to days later in the week. I never do strength training two days in a row, and I always take two consecutive days off during the week for my body to rest and my muscles to restore themselves. (If you are doing serious bodybuilding, you should take at least 72 hours between workouts).

I now do three sets of 15 reps on each area of the body I work. I do two different exercises for each of my major muscle groups: arms, legs, back, shoulders, chest, legs, and abdomen. I do one for each of the smaller groups: forearms, calves, inner and outer abductors, hamstrings, triceps, and glutes.

I continually increase the amount of weight I use for each of the exercises I do. However, since I am only toning, I usually increase the weight by two to two and one half pounds at a time, and I only increase two exercises per session. This approach challenges my body, but it also keeps me enjoying my workouts. Many excellent books show various exercises for working different areas of your body. I highly recommend starting with Larry North's *Living Lean* (1997).

The Challenge

You have the "why's" and you have my story. Now it's time for you to make your own decision. Please decide to commit to an exercise program.

Until two years ago, I was only committed as time allowed. Too often I would find myself pressed for a deadline or getting up so early to catch a flight that I'd have to forego my workout. Before I knew it, I would have only worked out three times in a week instead of the five to six workouts I was committed to.

I finally realized that taking care of myself and my body was more important than any deadline or other project that might appear in my life. I am often teased by friends and family who say: "She doesn't miss, and she doesn't cheat." If I am running with someone and we get back to the starting point three minutes early, I simply run in place for three minutes. I run in the rain; I get up before the chickens when necessary, and *I make time!*

I want you to feel as great as I do! I appeared on a radio show in Detroit this morning via phone from Dallas. The interviewer had seen me in person a month ago when I spoke to a group in Novi, Michigan, just outside Detroit. She told the audience today: "I wish this was a television interview so you could see this lady. She has been telling you that she feels great, but I'm here to tell you she looks great too! She radiates vitality!" Now isn't it interesting that the very words that inspired my commitment to exercise came back to me!

I hope something in this chapter has inspired you and that you will make a commitment to yourself! Then share it with someone else so that you can be accountable! I wish you the gift of feeling as great as I do!

Write your commitment to exercise here. Start slow if you would like, but as Nike taught us: "Just do it!"

_____

_____

_____

_____

_____

_____

_____

_____

Chapter 3

The Case for Recreation

Re-creating ourselves regularly through fun, laughter, and playful behavior is absolutely essential for a life of high level wellness.

The Bible actually communicates this sentiment perfectly: "A cheerful heart is good medicine, but a crushed spirit dries up the bones" (*NIV,* Proverbs 17:22).

The word *recreation* can actually be broken with a hyphen to create the word *re-creation.* Often when we talk or think about recreation, recess in school comes to mind. We may think of children playing on a playground. However, recreation is just as important for adults as it is for children.

We have all become so busy, myself included. I occasionally have to remind myself to take a break and to re-create myself. When I do, my progress and creativity skyrocket!

Just this afternoon, I had been sitting at the computer for hours, researching and writing. My back had begun to ache, and I felt I'd never get this book completed. I took a break and went out to the barn to feed my horses. Instead of being on a mission and running straight back to the computer, I decided to spend some time with them. I got some watermelon, and started feeding them an extra treat. My horses love watermelon. They came over and took some from my hand, and then ran and played. Then they came back for more.

I climbed up on the fence and played with Sundance, my treasured paint. Soon Chocolate Drop, Buck, and Dakota also wanted some extra lovin'. I laughed as Chocolate Drop tried to eat a piece of watermelon that had fallen to the ground. She wanted it so badly, but it was covered with dirt. She would pick it up in her mouth, then spit it out and cough. Before I knew it, I was feeling refreshed. When I came back inside, a particularly difficult passage of writing just flowed!

Recreation, or time for fun, is so important!

One of the most delightful books I came across in graduate school was *Taming Your Gremlin: A Guide to Enjoying Yourself* (Carson, 1983). He talks about the gremlins within us that attempt to steal our ability to have fun. In one part of the book, he identifies the myths the gremlins tell us. Among them are:

* You can only enjoy yourself for short periods of time.
* Fast is good and slow is bad.
* Worry has value.
* Anxiety has value.
* Guilt has value.
* To express uncensored joy is to be silly or unprofessional.

I know that I have had a gremlin alive and well in me that kept me from enjoying myself far too often along the way. Although I am dedicated to my work (and love my work), I have learned to take breaks for joy and fun on the journey!

Work Addiction

Work addiction is one of the greatest robbers of recreation in our time. This condition is difficult to identify, because we are rewarded for hard work, for dedication to our work, for long work hours. A prolific author (who also happens to be a good friend of mine) Dr. Bryan Robinson (1989) describes work addiction accurately and succinctly by calling it "the disease that kisses and kills" (24). He further writes about this disease: "It is the blessed betrayal. It's the only lifeboat guaranteed to sink" (24).

Research has shown the obsession with work to be very similar to other addictions. Characteristics include such things as identity issues, rigid thinking, withdrawal, progressive involvement and denial (Porter, 1996).

Other major signs of work addiction include (Robinson, 1989; Robinson and Post, 1997):

* hurrying and staying busy
* need for control
* perfectionism
* difficulty with relationships
* work binges
* difficulty relaxing and having fun
* impatience and irritability
* self-neglect
* poor communication
* lower overall family functioning

I am aware of this whole concept, because "I are one!" More accurately, I should say, "I am a recovering work addict." I'm not really sure when it started for me, but I know that I had fully succumbed by the time I was in my mid-20s. I was accomplishing more in a shorter period of time than many full office staffs were able to produce. I received lots of strokes for this behavior, and I loved the feeling of getting things done. Soon my hours became longer; my fuse became shorter; and my need for perfection became greater.

I'm very grateful for the "bottoming-out" experience I had that helped me clear the decks. I had a full-time practice. I conducted seminars and support groups several evenings a week. I was a partner in an outpatient treatment program for sexual abuse. I ran an inpatient program at a hospital in a neighboring city with my partner where we did all the weekend programs, and I was on part-time staff at my church.

I'll never forget the day everything came crashing in on me. I lived in a three-story townhome where my window opened onto an old train trestle that was no longer in use. One night, I dreamed that I heard an awful noise—a car crashed into the trestle, and people were killed. After the accident, some of the survivors who were barely alive were knocking on my door, begging for help. I desperately needed to rest, but I couldn't let them die. When I awakened, I was in a cold sweat.

I processed that dream with my therapist. I'll never forget the look on her face when she said, "I guess it's getting pretty close to home. Now you literally can't even rest in peace because your need to help and work is moving in on you." I knew she was right, but I wasn't sure what to do. So—you guessed it—I went back to work!

About a week later, as I was sleeping, I heard the same screeching brakes and awful crash that I had heard in my dream again, but this time I could have sworn it was real. I got up and went to the window, and there the scene was, just as I had dreamed it. I called 9-1-1, and ambulances and fire trucks arrived in less than a minute. As bodies were carried away and the fire trucks washed down the street hours later, I asked a policeman to check my patio. Sure enough, one of the inebriated passengers had crawled back to the door where I had dreamed the victims were knocking and had passed out.

This time, I didn't go back to work. This time, I got a vision of how short life is and how desperately I needed to have some fun. I honestly didn't know what to do, so I went to a weeklong seminar on recovery in Wickenburg, Arizona. At the seminar, my good friend

Pia Mellody helped me map out a plan of recovery from my work addiction.

First, I was to take five minutes a day for fun. Now you might think this funny, but I had no idea what fun was! I had forgotten how to have fun, how to laugh! I had forgotten how to re-create myself!

I quickly figured out that I could relax better on the beach than any place else on earth, so I got an apartment near the beach in Galveston and started taking a week off from work a month and going to just lay in the sun, read, build sand castles, and watch kids run and play. And so my recovery began.

Although I am still a hard worker, many people who know me have a hard time believing I was ever a work addict. When I feel myself crossing the line from hard work into a compulsion to work, I take a break. I go for a run. I take a long, hot bubble bath, I ride my horse—whatever it takes to have a moment of fun. And if I'm absolutely desperate, I can always get a laugh by flipping on *The Jerry Springer Show* for five minutes! Or I put on my favorite music and dance, dance, dance!

One thing is certain: You can't re-create yourself or have any fun when you are a work addict!

If you are a work addict, recovery is possible! My good friend, Dr. Bryan Robinson (1989, 137) sets the stage for the solution when he says: "Work is a substitute for the spiritual hunger that only recovery can satisfy." I think the first three steps of the 12-step program can be broken down into some very simple beliefs that can satisfy that spiritual hunger. I summarize them this way:

Step 1: I can't.
Step 2: He can.
Step 3: I think I'll let Him.

When you let Him take charge, you will find time for fun and re-creation in your life!

The Healing Power of Joy and Laughter

Laughter and joy are great eradicators of stress, and they are actually very healing! When I think about laughter, I get a picture of my Mamaw "laughing all over!" She would laugh and rock and hold her sides, such a jolly laugh. I remember one of her best laughs. I think I was in the second grade. We were preparing for Christmas at school, and our class had cut little angels out of construction paper. We made a circle with their skirts and taped it at the back so that they would stand up. We then put glitter on their wings and attached them with glue. Then we took some of our school pictures and put our faces on the angels. I took mine home, and when Mamaw saw me as a little angel, it hit her funny bone. She laughed and cackled until she could hardly sit in the chair.

In his book *The Peter Principle*, Dr. Laurence Peter (1996) details how laughing actually reduces the tension caused by stress. Because it is impossible to feel tense during laughter, laughter actually eradicates stress (Wooten, 1996). The bigger the laugh, the lower our tension, and consequently, the longer our relief from stress lasts. Following laughter, our body tension can continue in a reduced state for up to an hour (Peter and Hull, 1996).

Although the past twenty years have shed new light on the use of laughter in healing as demonstrated by medical research, the use of laughter in the healing process is nothing new. As far back as the early 1200s,

Dr. Henri de Mondeville, a professor of surgery, wrote: "Let the surgeon take care to regulate the whole regimen of the patient's life for joy and happiness, allowing his relatives and special friends to cheer him, and by having someone tell him jokes" (Walsh, 1928).

Norman Cousins actually brought the whole concept of laughter and healing back to our attention in the 1960s. He was diagnosed with ankylosing spondylitis, a disease that inflames and stiffens the joints, making the spine rigid. Additional symptoms include extreme fatigue, lung disease, and chronic pain. Cousins decided that the disease would not take him down. Along with conventional medical treatment, he initiated a program of humor and "laughter therapy." He believes that it was his self-designed program of telling jokes, listening to jokes, and watching slapstick movies that healed him (Cousins, 1976).

Researchers at Loma Linda University School of Medicine in California set out to discover whether there were actual biochemical reactions in the body when a person laughs. They began their research with a small group of ten healthy males. They ran lab tests before and after laughter was induced by humorous videos on half the participants. The other half of the study participants did not view the video. Results were fairly astonishing: The laughter increased CD4 (T-helper) cell counts and natural killer cell activity. The laughter session also activated antibodies and gamma interferon, which are all-important parts of a healthy immune system. The laughter session also suppressed stress hormones (cortisol, dopac, adrenaline) that are immunosuppressive (Berk et al., 1989).

When we are stressed, our adrenal glands produce corticosteroids, which quickly turn to stress hormones in the body. These stress hormones actually suppress our immune systems. Thus, we often become sick when we are stressed. Laughter actually stimulates the immune system, releasing T cells which counteract the immunosuppressive effects of stress (Berk, 1989).

When the specialized cells that attack microbial invaders are released, they not only reduce stress hormones and build up our immune systems, but they also fight any cancer cells present (Rensberger, 1997).

The benefits of laughter are really immense. I think you could say that laughter is good for the soul!

Laughter has been scientifically shown to reduce muscle tension and to stimulate the heart and lungs. Laughter causes the diaphragm, the main muscle of respiration, to work heavily. Deep respiration that accompanies hearty laughter increases the oxygen level in the blood. Norman Cousins, editor and author turned laughter researcher, has called laughter a form of internal jogging. Thus, it has particular benefits to those who have been physically inactive due to long-term illness. Laughter increases the production of endorphins, natural painkillers created within the body and of disease-fighting antibodies. Laughter and humor may also play a part in increased longevity (Heidorn, 1996).

Laughter really does have the power to reduce pain. One study measured the pain threshold of both men and women before and after a laughter session. The study revealed that the threshold for pain increased substantially following laughter conditioning, indicating that laughter truly has pain-relieving qualities (Cogan et al., 1987).

At my house, we've had lots of dental appointments through the summer. Although we all love our dentist, no one really likes getting cavities filled and other fun things like having wisdom teeth pulled. As my daughter was going in for a session, she looked at me and said, "I know: Laugh, baby, laugh!"

There are various other benefits to laughter. One is that it actually increases the metabolism and activity of our muscles and thereby improves the condition of our musculature, including our heart muscle (Fry, 1998). Laughter has also been shown to be lifesaving when used with depressed and suicidal elderly patients (Richman, 1995).

The United States spends approximately $23 billion annually to treat stress-related illnesses and diseases. A good laugh could cut these costs drastically. Not only does laughter relieve stress, it raises energy levels, wards off criticism and builds team spirit (Paquet, 1993).

So one of the best things you can do is to laugh, laugh, laugh! I was chatting via instant mail with my niece, Rebekah, the other day. She said something that made me laugh out loud. I said something funny back and she responded, "LOL!" She informed me that meant "laughing out loud." Then to something else funny, she responded, "ROFL" ("Rolling On the Floor Laughing"). The last one was "LMBO," which means "Laughing My B___ Off!" So there's even a healing vocabulary floating around on the Internet.

The Challenge

Re-creating ourselves regularly through fun, laughter, and playful behavior is absolutely essential for a life of high level wellness. Make your commitment to laughing and playing right now. Share your commitment with your friends. They will probably be delighted and would just love to join in on some of the fun!

Write your commitment to re-creation, fun and laughter here:

_____

_____

_____

_____

_____

Chapter 4

The Case for Healthful Being, Eating and Loving

Prayer was so deeply rooted in me that nothing and no one has been able to shake my beliefs about prayer anywhere along my life's journey.

When I address audiences and relate my personal regimen as I've so far reported it to you, someone invariably raises her hand and asks: "Is that all?" Actually, there's more.

You have probably noted that I have not addressed specifics about food, nutritional intake, and weight loss. These topics would encompass an entire book.

Your might then ask: "When is *that* book coming out?" I would answer that it's not the next book on my agenda, but I do hope to write such a treatment someday.

Research in this area is advancing and changing very quickly, and some of the data is so compelling that I am rethinking my own approach to food and nutritional intake.

Finally, I think that often we tend to focus on food too much, to the exclusion of other more important healthful practices that I have focused on in this book.

There are a handful of other points that I believe to be crucial parts of my high level wellness.

Healthful Being—Prayer and Meditation

I learned the power of prayer as a toddler. As a matter of fact, prayer was so deeply rooted in me that nothing and no one has been able to shake my beliefs about prayer anywhere along my life's journey.

I was probably three years old when my belief took root. My dad owned a Texaco gas station in Dangerfield, Texas. I don't remember much about that time in my life, but I do remember always being so proud to see my dad when we would go visit him there.

One evening we visited my father at work on our way to the drive-in theatre, a rare treat for us as a rather poor family. The windshield of our old car was being washed so that we could have a clear view of the movie. (I'm sure a clean windshield mattered little to me, because shortly after the cartoon, I was sure to be fast asleep!)

In any event, we never made it to the movies that evening. Somehow, my thumb got caught in the gears of the machine that wrung the water from the chamois used for cleaning the windshield. My parents rushed me to the hospital where doctors attempted to put my little mangled, dangling thumb back together.

Days later, when infection had set in from the grease, the doctors announced to my mother that they felt sure my thumb needed to be amputated to preserve the rest of my hand.

My mother had in her then the same deep-rooted belief about prayer I've come to have. She rushed home and called the person she believed to have the most direct route to heaven, my Mamaw. Mamaw immediately began praying and rushed to our little town. My grandmother also believed in the "laying on of hands" and praying: She wanted to hold my little hopeless thumb in her hands.

I remember only that the next day when we went to see the doctors, they couldn't imagine what had happened. Today, that thumb is very much intact with only scars to remind me that I once almost lost it. Each time I see them, the scars remind me of the power of prayer!

Healing through prayer is nothing new. Every culture, country, and civilization has engaged in this practice since the beginning of time (Whitmont, 1993). A 1996 poll by *Time* magazine revealed that 73 percent of Americans believe praying for someone can effectively influence their health (Stryker, 1998).

Science can no longer turn its back on these healings: By the early 1990s, at least 56 scientific studies have significantly connected prayer and healing (Targ, 1997).

A tremendous study was conducted at the San Francisco General Hospital in the mid-1980s. The study involved 393 patients in the coronary care unit.

For the test group, a Christian prayer circle received the first names of individual patients and their diagnoses. The circle prayed for this group daily. The circle did not pray for individuals in the second group. The study findings were remarkable: The patients for whom the group prayed had significantly fewer complications than normal, decreased incidence of pneumonia, reduced need for antibiotics and lessened severity of disease (Byrd, 1988).

Another study employed 53 male patients who had experienced hernia surgery. The patients were divided into three groups: One group listened to tapes featuring positive thoughts about a quick recovery; a group unknown to them prayed for the second group; and the third group received medical treatment only. The group receiving the prayers experienced improved healing of their wounds, had less fever, less pain, and more confidence in their treatment (Bentwich and Kreitler, 1994).

Prayer as treatment for hypertensive patients has also been researched. One study involved three groups: The first was prayed for by the laying on of hands. Prayers were offered from a distance for members of a second group; and the third group received no spiritual intervention. At the conclusion of the study, both groups who had received the prayers exhibited significant decreases in blood pressure (Beutler et al., 1988).

Dr. Elizabeth Targ, clinical director of psychosocial oncology research at California Pacific Medical Center in San Francisco, conducted a study with AIDS patients. In the study, 20 severely ill individuals were prayed for; 20 others were not (Wallis, 1996). The results were fascinating: Although some of the groups offering prayers for the patients were as far away as Alaska and Puerto Rico, the patients in whose names the prayers were offered experienced fewer hospitalizations and fewer doctor visits than the patients for whom no prayers were offered (Stryker, 1998).

David Larson, who is a well-known researcher in the area of healing prayer and medicine, conducted a survey among patients. He found that 75 percent believed their doctors should be concerned about their spiritual needs, and about 50 percent wanted their doctors to pray for them (Fleming, 1997).

Why are physicians and scientists becoming more interested in prayer? Because patients believe in prayer and its power to heal. Just a few years ago, very few medical schools paid any attention to spirituality and healing. Because of new research and patient demand, more than 50 North American medical schools are considering the addition of courses related to spirituality and healing (Devine, 1998).

The time has come for the medical community to acknowledge prayer and healing, and for us to pray for the health of others and ourselves.

My Prayer Regimen

I am a Christian, and I pray every morning while I am working out. Through the marvelous instruction of Dr. Larry Lea, I learned to pray using the Lord's Prayer as an outline. I believe prayer works!

Once again, I was reminded vividly of the power of prayer almost seven years ago. My mother was diagnosed with ovarian cancer and was immediately scheduled for a radical hysterectomy. After she'd been in surgery for several hours, my mother's wonderful surgeon, Dr. Sterling Sightler, came out to inform my dad, my sister and me that my mother's condition was indeed cancerous. My sister and my dad both crumbled in sobs, but somehow I was able to look down at my thumb, to remember, and to pray.

After a miraculous recovery from surgery—one that matched women less than half her age—my mother took one chemotherapy treatment. She was incredibly sick from the procedure, and after much thought and prayer, she announced to the family that she was going to refuse further chemotherapy and trust God.

She has now been cancer-free for almost seven years! I believe in prayer!

Healthful Eating

I want to start by making a huge proclamation here: *I do not diet!* And I hope you don't either!

I do, however, have some specific guidelines governing how I eat. Since the subtitles of all of my books start with "The Facts about…" I have become known as the "Fact Lady." However, you would be very surprised how many people meet me and say, "You know, you're not *fat* at all." I have to explain that it's the *Fact* Lady, not the *Fat* Lady!

I am not fat; I do not diet; and I love to eat! You can have all of that too by following some specific guidelines.

First of all, I do not eat or drink *any* sugar!

I started this regimen quite by accident. I was running an alcohol treatment program at a local hospital. We always removed all sugar from the diets of inpatient drug addicts and alcoholics because sugar processes in the body much as alcohol does. One afternoon I was writing in a chart when two of the young male patients came to the desk, harassing me about the absence of sugar from their diets. They moaned and groaned and begged, "You don't know how hard it is. This isn't fair! It's almost Thanksgiving."

Since the normal length of stay for the program was two to four weeks and both patients had been in the unit almost two weeks, I felt safe to make a deal with them. I said, "Okay, if you will cut the whining, I promise you that I will eat *no* sugar as long as you are here. We'll suffer together." They loved the idea!

Well, wouldn't you know that one of them ended up staying almost twelve weeks? I kept my promise, and I missed all the wonderful sweets of both Thanksgiving and Christmas. But two things happened that got my attention:

1) I stopped having headaches.
2) That afternoon nap that crawled

up on my shoulder daily, lulling me into never-never land disappeared!

I vowed then to remove all sugar from my diet.

Although it was not popular almost ten years ago when I first adopted this regimen, there are many books and articles about it now. As a matter of fact, *Sugar Busters* (Steward et al., 1998) is an entire book devoted to the topic. Steward relates adamantly that sugar is toxic and makes us fat!

When I tell people that abstaining from sugar is part of my regimen, they often say, "That's no big deal, I'm not that fond of sweets anyway!" Before you think that you have this one mastered, let me clarify.

Sugar is not just what you eat in ice cream and candy bars; sugar appears in many processed foods we eat, foods like ketchup, barbecue sauce, salad dressing.

In addition, many foods you would never connect to sugar turn to sugar almost immediately once they begin the process of digestion. Dr. Bob Arnot (1997) wrote an excellent book, *Dr. Bob Arnot's Revolutionary Weight Control Program,* about how quickly many foods turn to sugar. He uses the term "glucose load" or "glycemic index" to determine exactly how quickly foods turn to sugar in our bodies, raising our blood sugar levels.

When we eat too much of such food, our bodies go into glucose overload. In this condition we are at risk for diabetes, chronic fatigue, depression, obesity, hyperactivity, and many other diseases.

So if I'm not talking about Snickers and Cokes, what am I talking about? Foods with high glycemic indexes turn to sugar instantly: potatoes, white pasta, white bread, white rice, and corn.

I know, I know. You have read all the great information about how you need to load up on pasta and dry baked potatoes to be healthy. Dr. Arnot dispels this myth:

> Carbo-loading gained great popularity in the 1980s as a way for elite marathoners to run harder longer. Never in the history of nutrition has a good idea gone so wrong. Now most of America carbo loads every day at every meal. Sure, several hundred world-class marathoners benefited by crossing the finish line a few minutes faster, but tens of millions of carbo-overloaded Americans made their way into the history books as the fattest generation ever (Arnot, 1997, 67).

I don't know about you, but I don't want to be a number in that history book! The remedy is simple: eliminate all sugar!

You may be saying to yourself, "Now she's gone from delivering facts to meddling in my personal affairs." So I have! And you may protest further: "I could never do that! I'll starve to death!"

No you won't! Did you know that whole-wheat macaroni with tofu cheese and soymilk is better than the macaroni and cheese you can make out of a box? You can also find anything your heart desires to eat in a sugar-free edition.

Here's the challenge: resolve to do it for two weeks, just 14 days. See how you feel. I think you'll be willing to go the distance!

I have two more challenges for you in this area: Stop smoking and don't drink or eat caffeine. (Chocolate is full of caffeine, you know!)

I'll spare you of my smoking "soap box" and just give you a few facts. First and foremost *smoking kills!*

These deaths are preventable! All you have to do is stop smoking!

> Tobacco use is the most important single preventable cause of death and disease in our society. Tobacco use is a major risk factor for diseases of the heart and blood vessels; chronic bronchitis and emphysema; cancers of the lung, larynx, pharynx, oral cavity, esophagus, pancreas, and bladder; and other problems such as respiratory infections and stomach ulcers (Public Health, 1998).

Cigarette smoking accounts for one fifth of all deaths in the United States (Herdman et al., 1993). According to the Surgeon General, "Smoking represents the most extensively documented cause of disease ever investigated in the history of biomedical research" (US Department of Health and Human Services, 1990).

Smoking is not just a problem in the United States: Smoking kills worldwide! For the decade 1990-1999, researchers estimate that smoking will cause 21 million deaths in developed countries and that more than 50 percent of those deaths will befall people between the ages of 35 and 69. This statistic will make tobacco the largest single cause of premature death (Petro et al., 1992). Annual worldwide mortality from smoking is projected to exceed ten million during the early 2000s (Petro and Lopez, 1990).

End of soapbox. Please stop smoking!

I also have stopped all use of caffeine. "Caffeine is the most overused stimulant in the world" (Henner and Morton, 1998, 58). Numerous health risks are associated with caffeine, including hypertension, abnormal heart rates, miscarriages, birth defects (cleft palates, missing fingers and toes), infertility, ulcers, osteoporosis, panic attacks, acid indigestion, fibrous breast lumps, insomnia, and headaches just to name a few (Schardt and Schmidt, 1996).

Coffee specifically is a stimulant that really beats our central nervous system. This stimulation is like whipping an exhausted horse to make the beast do more. The animal may perform, but not without a price. Why would we do that to our own bodies? Just as with the horse, the more we whip them, the more we need to whip them to keep them going. The more caffeine you consume, the more you need to keep going! The cycle is endless, and you are merely wearing yourself out!

When I stopped all caffeine intake, I had the shakes and a terrible headache for a week. When I got through the withdrawal and a period of adjustment, I had more energy than ever before! I challenge you to find a way to "get yourself going" without the caffeine. You'd be amazed how effectively a vigorous walk or a gym workout will produce the same result!

Healthful Loving

I doubt you'll need too much convincing to make a commitment to this practice!

There are many different definitions for love and intimacy. According to *Webster's Dictionary* (1993,), love is "intense affection for another arising out of kinship or personal ties," and intimacy is "characterized by close friendship or association."

I've always loved the definition for love in the Bible found in I Corinthians 13:4-8.

> Love is patient, love is kind. It does not envy, it does not boast, it is not proud. It is not rude, it is not self-seeking, it is not easily angered, it keeps no record of wrongs. Love does not delight in evil but rejoices with the truth. It always protects, always trusts, always hopes, always perseveres. Love never fails. (*NIV*, 1985).

When I read that definition of love as an adolescent, I became very aware of the word *love*, and I also became cautious about its use!

Regardless of your personal definitions for love and intimacy, research strongly supports their healing power and their benefits in our lives.

A study of patients undergoing coronary angiography at Yale University revealed interesting results (Seeman and Syme, 1987). (This procedure shows degrees of blockage in the coronary arteries.) The study showed that patients who reported feeling more loved and emotionally supported had less coronary blockage.

Another study investigated 10,000 married male patients who had no history of chest pain. Unsurprisingly, the study found men with high levels of cholesterol, high blood pressure and diabetes were at least 20 times more likely to develop chest pain in the following five years. However, the study disclosed something interesting about those who felt loved by their wives. Even test subjects who had high risk factors were much less likely to experience chest pain. Those who claimed a wife who did not show her love were twice as likely to experience significant chest pain (Medalie and Goldbourt, 1976).

The same researchers studied about 8,500 men who had no history of stomach ulcers. During the five years following the study, 254 developed ulcers. Those who reported feeling unloved by their wives when the study began five years earlier were three times more likely to develop ulcers than those who felt loved (Medalie et al., 1992).

Parental love is a very important kind of love. Researchers at the University of Arizona in Tucson found that parental love and care reflected the core of social support in the first 20 years of a person's life. In the early 1950s, healthy undergraduate males at Harvard University described their relationships with their parents in childhood. Thirty-five years later a follow-up study was conducted with the same men. Ninety-five percent of those students who had characterized their parents as unloving in the earlier study had developed diseases in midlife. Only 29 percent of

those who had described their parents as loving had developed diseases in midlife. This result indicates that early parental love may be a special predictor of long-term health (Russek and Schwartz, 1996).

Love and support from friends and family can actually be life-saving. One researcher, Dr. Spiegel, initially set out to disprove that patients with metastatic breast cancer could be helped in a support group setting (Spiegel et al., 1989). There were 86 women in the study at Stanford University School of Medicine. For one year, 50 of the patients attended support groups weekly. The other 36 had only routine oncological care. The groups were followed up ten years later. Those who attended the support group lived twice as long as those who did not. All of the individuals who did not attend the support group were dead five years after the study. Dr. Spiegel was totally astonished when he reviewed the results. In his book, *Living Beyond Limits* (1993), he stated, "I finally got around to looking at the data, and I almost fell off my chair." Apparently, the results made a believer out of him!

I mentioned earlier that my mother is a seven-year survivor of ovarian cancer. Her oncologist is one who reads the latest research and gives her patients every advantage for regaining their health. She provides a support group for all of her patients, and my mother became involved in the group immediately following her diagnosis.

The group calls itself "The Pap Squad." I have been involved from a distance with the group for seven years now. Although I find the social worker who leads the group ineffective, the organization has a life of its own—and I emphasize the word *life*. Although they have lost dear members, the group stays alive and provides valuable support for each other, for other patients, and for their families.

I know that if I were diagnosed with breast or ovarian cancer, or if I were a family member of someone with the diagnosis, my mother is just the kind of person I would want to appear in my hospital room with a tender touch, a word of encouragement, and always a prayer!

Love is a great healer and an important aspect in all of our lives. I am so blessed to be surrounded by love! However, I have found that the greatest key to receiving love is to give love away. I remember taking the challenge given by the speaker at my high school graduation. He told us that we all had the capacity to go on and become great doctors, lawyers, executives, moms and dads. He added that the most important role we could ever assume—no matter what our profession—was to be a giver of love. He ended with the words to a song:

> A song's not a song til you sing it.
> A bell's not a bell til you ring it.
> Love wasn't put in your heart to stay.
> Love isn't love…til you give it away!

Make your decision and commitment to healthful being, eating and loving right now. Share that commitment with a friend. I can assure you that they will be delighted to be the object of your love! Write your commitment down right here…right now!

_____

_____

_____

_____

_____

_____

_____

Bibliography for High Level Wellness

Introduction

"Births, Marriages, Divorces, and Deaths." *Monthly Vital Statistics Report.* Volume 46, Number 1, June 1997, pages 98–1120.

Moore, Neecie. *Bountiful Health, Boundless Energy, Brilliant Youth: The Facts about DHEA.* Dallas, TX: Charis Publishing, 1994.

Moore, Neecie. *Designing Your Life with Designer Foods: The Facts about Phytochemicals.* Dallas, TX: Charis Publishing, 1996.

Moore, Neecie. *The Miracle in Aloe vera: The Facts about Polymannans.* Dallas, TX: Charis Publishing, 1995.

Moore, Neecie. *The Missing Link: The Facts about Glyconutrients.* Seattle, WA: Validation Press, 1997.

Staton, Bill. *The America's Finest Companies Investment Plan.* New York: Hyperion, 1998.

Thorpe, Kenneth E. "Changes in the Growth in Health Care Spending: Implications for Consumers." *Emerging Health Trends.* April 1997.

Chapter One – The Case for Nutritional Supplements

Adlercreutz, H. "Phytoestrogens: Epidemiology and a Possible Role in Cancer Protection." *Environ Health Perspect.* Volume 103, Number 7, October 1995, pages 103-112.

Allain, H., P. Raoul, A. Lieury, F. LeCoz, J.M. Gandon, and P. d'Arbigny. "Effect of Two Doses of Ginkgo Biloba Extract (Egb 761) on the Dual-Coding Test in Elderly Adults." *Clin Ther.* Volume 15, Number 3, May-June 1993, pages 549-558.

Andon, M.B., M. Peacock, R.L. Kanerva, and J.A. De Castro. "Calcium Absorption from Apple and Orange Juice Fortified with Calcium Citrate Malate (CCM)." *J Am Coll Nutr.* Volume 15, June 1996, pages 313-316.

Anthony, M.S., T.B. Clarkson, C.L. Hughes, Jr., T.M. Morgan, and G.L. Burke. "Soybean Isoflavones Improve Cardiovascular Risk Factors Without Affecting the Reproductive System of Peripubertal Rhesus Monkeys." *J Nutr.* Volume 126, Number 1, January 1996, pages 43-50.

Barnes, S. "Evolution of the Health Benefits of Soy Isoflavones." *Proc Soc Exp Biol Med.* Volume 217, March 1998, pages 386-392.

Birkmayer, J.G., C. Vrecko, D. Volc, and W. Birkmayer. "Nicotinamide Adenine Dinucleotide (NADH)—A Therapeutic Approach to Parkinson's Disease. Comparison of Oral and Parenteral Application." *Acta Neurol Scand Suppl.* Volume 146, 1993, pages 32-35.

Birkmayer, W. and J.G. Birkmayer. "The Coenzyme Nicotinamide Adenine Dinucleotide (NADH) as Biological Anti-Depressive Agent." *New Trends in Clinical Neuropharmacology.* Volume 5, 1991, pages 19-25.

Brandi, M.L. "Natural and Synthetic Isoflavones in the Prevention and Treatment of Chronic Diseases." *Calcif Tissue Int.* Volume 61, Number 1, 1997, pages 5-8.

Dean, Ward and John Morgenthaler. *Smart Drugs and Nutrients.* Santa Cruz, CA: B & J Publications, 1991.

Eisenberg, D.M., R.C. Kessler, C. Foster, F.E. Norlock, D.R. Calkins, and T.L. Delbanco. "Unconventional Medicine in the United States. Prevalence, Costs, and Patterns of Use." *New England Journal of Medicine.* Volume 328, Number 4, January 28, 1993, pages 246-252.

Freeman, J.W. and J. Landis. "Alternative/Complementary Therapies." *SDJ Med.* Volume 50, Number 2, February 1997, pages 65-66.

"Getting the Jump on Osteoporosis." *Harvard Women's Health Watch.* Volume 3, Number 5, January 1996, page 1.

Grassel, E. "Effect of Ginkgo-Biloba Extract on Mental Performance. Double-Blind Study Using Computerized Measurement Conditions in Patients with Cerebral Insufficiency." *Fortschr Med.* Volume 110, Number 5, February 20, 1992, pages 73-76.

Herman, C., T. Adlercreutz, B.R. Goldin, S.L. Gorbach, K.A. Hockerstedt, S. Watanabe, E.K. Hamalainene, M.H. Markkanen, T.H. Makela, and K.T. Wahala. "Soybean Phytoestrogen Intake and Cancer Risk." *J Nutr.* Volume 125, Number 3, March 1995, pages 757-770.

Horn-Ross, P.L. "Phytoestrogens, Body Composition, and Breast Cancer." *Cancer Causes Control.* Volume 6, November 1995, pages 567-573.

Ishida, H., T. Uesugi, K. Hirai, T. Toda, H. Nukaya, K. Yokotsuka, and K. Tsuji. "Preventive Effects of the Plant Isoflavones, Daidzin and Genistin, on Bone Loss in Ovariectomized Rats Fed a Calcium-Deficient Diet." *Biol Pharm Bull.* Volume 21, January 1998, pages 62-66.

Itil, T. and D. Martorano. "Natural Substances in Psychiatry (Ginkgo biloba in Dementia)." *Psychopharmacol Bull.* Volume 31, Number 1, 1995, pages 147-158.

Jibrin, J. "Calcium Supplements Made Simple." *Prevention.* Volume 49, Number 3, March 1997, pages 81-85, 159-160.

Kamen, Betty. *Hormone Replacement Therapy: Yes or No?* Novato, CA: Nutrition Encounter, Inc., 1993.

Klatz, R. and C. Kahn. *Grow Young with Hgh.* Chicago, IL: World Health Network Publications, 1997.

Lawren, B. "The Hormone that Makes Your Body 20 Years Younger." *Longevity.* Volume 2, Number 12, October 1990, pages 31-34, 36.

Leblhuber, F., C. Neubauer, M. Peichi, F. Reisecker, F.X. Steinpartz, E. Windhager, and E. Dienstl. "Age and Sex Differences of Dehydroepiandrosterone Sulfate (DHEAS) and Cortisol (CRT) Plasma Levels in Normal Controls and Alzheimer's Disease." *Psychopharmacology.* Volume 111, 1993, pages 23-26.

Moore, Neecie. *Designing Your Life with Designer Foods: The Facts about Phytochemicals.* Dallas, TX: Charis Publishing, 1996.

Moore, Neecie. *The Miracle in Aloe vera: The Facts about Polymannans.* Dallas, TX: Charis Publishing, 1995.

Moore, Neecie. *The Missing Link: The Facts about Glyconutrients.* Seattle, WA: Validation Press, 1997.

O'Donnell, Jayne. "Neither Food Nor Drug." *USA Today.* June 19, 1997, page 1A.

"Optimal Calcium Intake." *National Institutes of Health Consensus Development Conference Statement.* June 6-8, 1994. NIH Consensus Statement Online at http://llisis.nlm.nih.gov/nih/cdc/www/97txt.html.

Ranelli, P.L., R.N. Dickerson, and K.G. White. "Use of Vitamin and Mineral Supplements by Pharmacy Students." *Am J Hosp Pharm.* Volume 50, Number 4, April 1993, pages 674-678.

Roberts, E. "Dehydroepiandrosterone (DHEA) and Its Sulfate (DHEA-S) as Neural Facilitators: Effects on Brain Tissue in Culture and on Memory in Young and Old Mice. A Cyclic GMP Hypothesis of Action of DHEA and DHEAS in Nervous System and Other Tissues." In *The Biologic Role of Dehydroepiandrosterone (DHEA).* M. Kalimi and W. Regelson, eds. New York: Walter De Gruyter, 1990, pages 13-42.

Ruiz-Larrea, M.B., A.R. Mohan, G. Paganga, N.J. Miller, G.P. Bolwell, and C.A. Rice-Evans. "Antioxidant Activity of Phytoestrogenic Isoflavones." *Free Radic Res.* Volume 26, January 1997, pages 63-70.

Slesinski, M.J., A.F. Subar, and L.L. Kahle. "Dietary Intake of Fat, Fiber and other Nutrients Is Related to the Use of Vitamin and Mineral Supplements in the United States: The 1992 National Health Interview Survey." *J Nutr.* Volume 126, Number 12, December 1996, pages 3001-3008.

Sobal, J. and L.F. Marquart. "Vitamin/Mineral Supplement Use Among Athletes: A Review of the Literature." *Intl J Sport Nutr.* Volume 4, Number 4, December 1994, pages 320-334.

Solimini, C. "Forever Young? Some Researchers Say Growth Hormones Can Turn Back the Clock." *Living Fit.* March/April 1996, pages 38-39.

Stephens, F.O. "Breast Cancer: Aetiological Factors and Associations (A Possible Protective Role of Phytoestrogens)." *Aust N Z J Surg.* Volume 67, November 1997, pages 755-760.

Stephens, F.O. "Phytoestrogens and Prostate Cancer: Possible Preventive Role." *Med J Aust.* Volume 167, August 4, 1997, pages 138-140.

United States Department of Agriculture, Human Nutrition Info. Services. *Food Guide Pyramid.* Leaflet #572, 1992.

Warot, D., L. Lacomblez, P. Danjou, E. Weiller, C. Payan, and A.J. Puech. "Comparative Effects of Ginkgo Biloba Extracts on Psychomotor Performances and Memory in Healthy Subjects." *Therapie.* Volume 46, Number 1, January-February 1991, pages 33-36.

"Yes, But WHICH Calcium Supplement?" *Tufts University Health and Nutrition Letter.* Volume 14, Number 12, February 1997, pages 4-5.

Zerwekh, J.E., P. Padalino, and C.Y. Pak. "The Effect of Intermittent Slow-Release Doeium Fluoride and Continuous Calcium Citrate Therapy on Calcitropic Hormones, Biochemical Markers of Bone Metabolism, and Blood Chemistry in Postmenopausal Osteoporosis." *Calcif Tissue Int.* Volume 61, October 1997, pages 272-278.

Chapter Two — The Case for Exercise

Arida, R.M., M.G. Naffah-Mazzacoratti, J. Soares, and E.A. Cavalheiro. "Effect of an Aerobic Exercise Program on Blood Pressure and Catecholamines in Normotensive and Hypertensive Subjects." *Braz J Med Biol Res.* Volume 29, May 1996, pages 633-637.

Bennett, S. "Cardiovascular Risk Factors in Australia: Trends in Socioeconomic Inequalities." *J Epidemiol Community Health.* Volume 49, 1995, pages 363-372.

Bung, P. and R. Artal. "Gestational Diabetes and Exercise: A Survey." *Semin Perinatol.* Volume 20, Number 4, August 1996, pages 328-333.

Canadian News Wire. "'Uh Oh Canada' National Survey Finds Canadians Overweight and Confused About It." December 1, 1997.

"Case Study: City of Glasgow." WHO Regional Office for Europe. July 20, 1998. Found on Internet at **http://www.who.dk.tech.hcp/cases/glasgowt.html**.

Courneya, K.S. and C.M. Friedenreich. "Relationship Between Exercise Pattern Across the Cancer Experience and Current Quality of Life in Colorectal Cancer Survivors." *J Altern Complement Med.* Volume 3, Number 3, Fall 1997, pages 215-226.

Coyle, C.P. and M.C. Santiago. "Aerobic Exercise Training and Depressive Symptomatology in Adults with Physical Disabilities." *Arch Phys Med Rehabil.* Volume 76, Number 7, July 1995, pages 647-652.

Cullinen, K. and M. Caldwell. "Weight Training Increases Fat-Free Mass and Strength in Untrained Young Women." *J Am Diet Assoc.* Volume 98, April 1998, pages 414-418.

Cummings, S.R., S.M. Rubin, and D. Black. "The Future of Hip Fractures in the United States. Numbers, Costs, and Potential Effects of Postmenopausal Estrogen." *Clin Orthop.* Volume 252, 1990, pages 163-166.

"Depression: What It Is and How to Get Help." *Washingtonian.* February 1994.

Dimeo, F., B.G. Rumberger, and J. Keul. "Aerobic Exercise as Therapy for Cancer Fatigue." *Med Sci Sports Exerc.* Volume 30, Number 4, April 1998, pages 475-478.

Duncan, K., S. Harris, and C.M. Ardies. "Running Exercise May Reduce Risk for Lung and Liver Cancer by Inducing Activity of Antioxidant and Phase II Enzymes." *Cancer Letters.* Volume 116, Number 2, June 24, 1997, pages 151-158.

Eriksson, J., S. Taimela, K. Eriksson, S. Parviainen, J. Peltonen, and U. Kujala. "Resistance Training in the Treatment of Non-Insulin-Dependent Diabetes Mellitus." *Int J Sports Med.* Volume 18, Number 4, May 1997, pages 242-246.

Ermalinski, R., P.G. Hanson, B. Lubin, J.I. Thornby, and P.A. Nahormek. "Impact of a Body-Mind Treatment Component on Alcoholic Patients." *J Psychosoc Nurs Ment Health Serv.* Volume 35, Number 7, July 1997, pages 39-45.

Ewart, C.K., D.R. Young, J.M. Hagbert. "Effects of School-Based Aerobic Exercise on Blood Pressure in Adolescent Girls at Risk for Hypertension." *Am J Public Health.* Volume 88, June 1998, pages 949-951.

"Exercise As Therapy." August 30, 1998. Found on the Internet at http://www.depression.com/anti/anit_23_exercise.html.

"Exercise Can Go To Your Head." *Consumer Reports on Health.* Volume 7, Number 9, September 1995, pages 104-105.

Fahey, P.J., E.T. Stallkamp, S. Kwatra. "The Athlete with Type I Diabetes: Managing Insulin, Diet and Exercise." *Am Fam Physician.* Volume 53, Number 5, April 1996, pages 1611-1624.

Friendenreich, C.M. and K.S. Courneya. "Exercise as Rehabilitation for Cancer Patients." *Clin J Sport Med.* Volume 6, Number 4, October 1996, pages 237-244.

Hata, K., T. Hata, K. Miyazaki, H. Kunishi, and J. Masuda. "Effect of Regular Aerobic Exercise on Cerebrovascular Tone in Young Women." *J Ultrasound Med.* Volume 17, Number 2, February 1998, pages 133-136.

"Historic Surgeon General's Report Offers New View of Moderate Physical Activity." Centers for Disease Control. July 1996. Found on Internet at http://www.cdc.gov/od/oc/media/pressrel/exerc12.htm.

"How Much Does Depression Cost Society?" *Harvard Mental Health Letter.* October 1994.

Iyawe, V.I., A.D. Ighoroje, and H.O. Iyawe. "Changes in Blood Pressure and Serum Cholesterol Following Exercise Training in Nigerian Hypertensive Subjects." *J Hum Hypertens.* Volume 10, Number 7, July 1996, pages 483-487.

Jin, P. "Changes in Heart Rate, Noradrenaline, Cortisol, and Mood During Tai Chi." *J Psychosomatic Research.* Volume 33, 1989, page 197-199.

Kano, K. "Relationship Between Exercise and Bone Mineral Density Among Over 5,000 Women Aged 40 Years and Above." *J Epidemiol.* Volume 8, March 1998, pages 28-32.

Lavie, C.J. and R.V. Milani. "Effects of Cardiac Rehabilitation and Exercise Training in Obese Patients with Coronary Artery Disease." *Chest.* Volume 109, Number 1, January 1996, pages 52-56.

Levine, M.D., M.D. Marcus, and P. Moulton. "Exercise in the Treatment of Binge Eating Disorder." *Int J Eat Disord.* Volume 19, Number 2, March 1993, pages 171-177.

"Lifestyles." *Exercise and Sport.* August 30, 1998. Found on the Internet at http://www.who.dk/country/swi/swih104.htm.

McAuley E., S.L. Mihalko, and S.M. Bane. "Exercise and Self-Esteem in Middle-Aged Adults: Multidimensional Relationships and Physical Fitness and Self-Efficacy Influences." *J Behav Med.* Volume 20, Number 1, February 1997, pages 67-83.

McFarling, U.L. "Out of the Blues." *Walking.* Volume 12, Number 6, November/December 1997, pages 55-59, 107, 111.

McTiernan, A., J.L. Stanford, N.S. Weiss, J.R. Daling, and L.F. Voigt. "Occurrence of Breast Cancer in Relation to Recreational Exercise in Women Age 50-64 Years." *Epidemiology.* Volume 7, Number 6, November 1996, pages 598-604.

Madsen, K.L., W.C. Adams and M.D. Van Loan. "Effects of Physical Activity, Body Weight and Composition, and Muscular Strength on Bone Density in Young Women." *Med Sci Sports Exerc.* Volume 30, January 1998, pages 114-120.

Mock, V., K.H. Dow, C.J. Meares, P.M. Grimm, J.A. Dienemann, M.E. Haisfield-Wolfe, W. Quitasol, S. Mitchell, A. Chakravarthy, and I. Gage. "Effects of Exercise on Fatigue, Physical Functioning, and Emotional Distress During Radiation Therapy for Breast Cancer." *Oncol Nurs Forum.* Volume 24, Number 6, July 1997, pages 991-1000.

Mosher, P.E., M.S. Nash, A.C. Perry, A.R. LaPerriere, and R.B. Goldberg. "Aerobic Circuit Exercise Training: Effect on Adolescents with Well-Controlled Insulin-Dependent Diabetes Mellitus." *Arch Phys Med Rehabil.* Volume 79, Number 6, June 1998, pages 652-657.

Nelson, M.E., M.A. Fiatarone, C.N.M. Morganti, I. Trice, R.A. Greenberg, and W.J. Evans. "Effects of High-Intensity Strength Training on Multiple Risk Factors for Osteoporotic Fractures." *JAMA.* Volume 272, 1994, pages 1909-1914.

Nelson, Miriam E. and Sarah Wernick. *Strong Women Stay Slim.* New York, NY: Bantam Books, 1998.

Neuberger, G.B., A.N. Press, H.B. Lindsley, R. Hinton, P.E. Cagle, K. Carlson, S. Scott, J. Dahl, and B. Kramer. "Effects of Exercise on Fatigue, Aerobic Fitness, and Disease Activity Measured in Persons with Rheumatoid Arthritis." *Res Nurs Health.* Volume 20, Number 3, June 1997, pages 195-204.

"New Survey Details Surprising Barriers to the Treatment of Depression." *Medical and Other News.* April 16, 1996. Found on the Internet at **http://www.ps/group.com/dg/78d2.htm.**

Nicolosi, Michelle. "The Depression Trap." *Orange County Register.* February 19, 1997.

Niebauer, J., R. Hambrecht, T. Velich, K. Hauer, C. Marburger, B. Kalberer, C. Weiss, E. von Hodenberg, G. Schierf, G. Schuler, R. Zimmermann, and W. Kubler. "Attenuated Progression of Coronary Artery Disease after Six Years of Multifactorial Risk Intervention: Role of Physical Exercise." *Circulation.* Volume 86, Number 8, October 21, 1997, pages 2534-2541.

Nolte, L.J., C.A. Nowson, and A.C. Dyke. "Effect of Dietary Fat Reduction and Increased Aerobic Exercise on Cardiovascular Risk Factors." *Clin Exp Pharmacol Physiol.* Volume 24, Number 11, November 1997, pages 901-903.

Noreau, L., H. Martineau, L. Roy, and M. Belzile. "Effects of a Modified Dance-Based Exercise on Cardiorespiratory Fitness, Psychological State and Health Status of Persons with Rheumatoid Arthritis." *Am J Phys Med Rehabil.* Volume 74, Number 1, January/February 1995, pages 19-27.

North, Larry. *Living Lean.* New York, NY: Fireside Books, 1997.

Oliveria S.A. and I.M. Lee. "Is Exercise Beneficial in the Prevention of Prostate Cancer?" *Sports Med.* Volume 23, Number 5, May 1997, pages 271-278.

Painter, Kim. "Help for Depression Not Being Utilized." *USA Today.* January 17, 1996.

Pronk, N.P., S.F. Crouse, and J.J. Rohack. "Maximal Exercise and Acute Mood Response in Women." *Physiol Behav.* Volume 57, Number 1, January 1995, pages 1-4.

"Psychological Consequences of Exercise and Sport." *Penn State.* Found on the Internet at **www.personal.psu.edu/faculty/s/m/sms18/kines321/ consequences.html**.

Robbins, Anthony. *Awaken the Giant Within.* New York, NY: Summit Books, 1991.

Ross, C.E. and D. Hayes. "Exercise and Psychologic Well-Being in the Community." *Am J Epidemiol.* Volume 127, Number 4, April 1988, pages 762-771.

Schwartz, A.L. "Patterns of Exercise and Fatigue in Physically Active Cancer Survivors." *Oncol Nurs Forum.* Volume 25, Number 3, April 1998, pages 485-491.

Scott, J.C. "Osteoporosis and Hip Fractures." *Rheum Dis Clin North Am.* Volume 16, Number 3, 1990, pages 717-740.

Segar, M.L., V.L. Katch, R.S. Roth, A.W. Garcia, T.I. Portner, S.G. Glickman, S. Haslanger, and E.G. Wilkins. "The Effect of Aerobic Exercise on Self-Esteem and Depressive and Anxiety Symptoms Among Breast Cancer Survivors." *Oncol Nurs Forum.* Volume 25, Number 1, January/February 1998, pages 107-113.

Shephard, R.J. and P.N. Shek. "Autoimmune Disorders, Physical Activity, and Training, with Particular Reference to Rheumatoid Arthritis." *Exerc Immunol Rev.* Volume 3, 1997, pages 53-67.

Shima, K., K. Shi, A. Mizuno, T. Sano, K. Ishida, and Y. Noma. "Exercise Training Has a Long-Lasting Effect on Prevention of Non-Insulin-Dependent Diabetes Mellitus in Otsuka-Long-Evans-Tokushima Fatty Rats." *Metabolism.* Volume 45, Number 4, April 1996, pages 475-480.

Shumway-Cook, A., W. Gruber, M. Baldwin, and S. Liao. "The Effect of Multidimensional Exercises on Balance, Mobility, and Fall Risk in Community-Dwelling Older Adults." *Phys Ther.* Volume 77, January 1997, pages 46-47.

Squires, Sally. "A Kick in the Pants from the Surgeon General." *Washington Post.* Tuesday, July 16, 1996, page Z11.

Van den Ende, C.H., J.M. Hazes, S. le Cessie, W.J. Mulder, D.G. Belfor, F.C. Breedveld, and B.A. Dijkmans. "Comparison of High and Low Intensity Training in Well Controlled Rheumatoid Arthritis. Results of a Randomized Clinical Trial." *Ann Thrum Dis.* Volume 55, Number 11, November 1996, pages 798-805.

Wallberg-Henriksson, H., J. Rincon, and J.R. Zierath. "Exercise in the Management of Non-Insulin-Dependent Diabetes Mellitus." *Sports Med.* Volume 25, Number 1, January 1998, pages 25-35.

Waterhouse, Debra. *Outsmarting the Female Fat Cell.* New York, NY: Warner Books, 1993.

"Why Are So Many Women Depressed?" *Women's Health.* Summer 1998.

Williams, P.T. "High-Density Lipoprotein Cholesterol and Other Risk Factors for Coronary Heart Disease in Female Runners." *N Engl J Med.* Volume 334, Number 20, May 16, 1996, pages 1298-1303.

Ytterberg, S.R., M.L. Mahowald, and H.E. Krug. "Exercise for Arthritis." *Baillieres Clin Rheumatol.* Volume 8, Number 1, February 1994, pages 161-189.

Chapter Three — The Case for Recreation

Barker, Kenneth, Gen. Ed. *NIV Study Bible: New International Version.* Grand Rapids, MI: Zondervan Publishing House, 1985.

Berk, L. "Eustress of Mirthful Laughter Modifies Natural Killer Cell Activity." *Clinical Research.* Volume 37, pages 115-117.

Berk, L.S., S.A. Tan, W.F. Fry, B.J. Napier, J.W. lee, R.W. Hubbard, J.E. Lewis, and W.C. Eby. "Neuroendocrine and Stress Hormone Changes During Mindful Laughter." *Am J Med Sci.* Volume 298, Number 6, December 1989, pages 390-396.

Carson, Richard. *Taming Your Gremlins: A Guide to Enjoying Yourself.* New York, NY: Harper & Row Publishers, 1983.

Cogan, R., D. Cogan, W. Wltz, and M. McCue. "Effects of Laughter and Relaxation on Discomfort Thresholds." *J Behav Med.* Volume 10, Number 2, pages 139-144.

Cousins, N. *Anatomy of an Illness.* New York, NY: W.W. Norton, 1979.

Fry, William. "The Power of Laughter." August 31, 1998.

Interview on Thrive@Health. Found on Internet at http://www.thriveonline.com/health/wfrychat.html.

Heidorn, Keith C. "Laugh Away Stress." *Living Gently Quarterly.* Fall 1996, pages 1-3.

Paquet, J.B. "Laughter and Stress Management in the OR." *Today's OR Nurse.* Volume 15, Number 6, November/December 1993, pages 13-17.

Peter, Laurence J. and Raymond Hull. *The Peter Principle.* New York, NY: Buccaneer Books, 1996.

Porter, G. "Organizational Impact of Workaholism: Suggestions for Researching the Negative Outcomes of Excessive Work." *J Occup Health Psychol.* Volume 1, Number 1, January 1996, pages 70-84.

Rensberger, Boyce. "But Seriously, Folks…What Is Laughter? Why Do We Do It?" *Washington Post.* September 10, 1997, page H-01.

Richman, J. "The Lifesaving Function of Humor with the Depressed and Suicidal Elderly." *Gerontologist.* Volume 35, Number 2, April 1995, pages 271-273.

Robinson, B.E. and P. Post. "Risk of Addiction to Work and Family Functioning." *Psychol Rep.* Volume 81, Number 1, August 1997, pages 91-95.

Robinson, Bryan E. *Work Addiction: Hidden Legacies of Adult Children.* Deerfield Beach, FL: Health Communications, Inc., 1989.

Walsh, J. *Laughter and Health.* New York: Appleton, 1928.

Wooten, P. "Humour: An Antidote for Stress." *Holist Nurs Pract.* Volume 10, Number 2, January 1996, pages 49-56.

Chapter Four – The Case for Healthful Being, Eating, and Loving

"April Indicator-of-the-Month: Tobacco Use." Public Health: Working for All of Us All of the Time. September 1, 1998. Found on the Internet at http://www.ak.org/haiapril.htm.

Arnot, Robert, M.D. *Dr. Bob Arnot's Revolutionary Weight Control Program.* New York, NY: Little, Brown, & Co., 1997.

Barker, Kenneth, Gen. Ed. *NIV Study Bible: New International Version.* Grand Rapids, MI: Zondervan Publishing House, 1985.

Bentwich, Z. and S. Kreitler. "Psychological Determinants of Recovery from Hernia Operations." Paper presented at Dead Sea Conference, June 1994, Tiberias, Israel.

Beutler, J.J., J.T.M. Attevelt, and S.A. Schouten. "Paranormal Healing and Hypertension. *Br Med J.* Volume 296, 1988, pages 1491-1494.

Byrd, R.C. "Positive Therapeutic Effects of Intercessory Prayer in a Coronary Care Unit Population." *South Med J.* Volume 81, Number 7, 1988, pages 826-829.

Devine, Nancy. "Prayer Video Takes on Its Own Life." *Anglican Journal.* April 1998.

Fleming, J.P. "A Prayer for the Ailing?" *Hippocrates.* Volume 11, Number 5, 1997, pages 24-28.

"Health Benefits of Smoking Cessation." US Department of Health and Human Services. Rockville, Maryland: Public Health Service, Centers for Disease Control, Center for Chronic Disease Prevention and Health Promotion, Office on Smoking and Health, 1990. DHHS Publication No (CDC) 90-8416.

Henner, Marilu and Laura Morton. *Total Health Makeover*. New York, NY: Regan Books, 1998.

Herdman, R., M. Hewitt, and M. Saschober. *Smoking-Related Deaths and Financial Costs: Office of Technology Assessment Estimates for 1990*. OTA testimony before the Senate Special Committee on Aging, May 6, 1993.

Medalie, J.H. and U. Goldbourt. "Angina Pectoris among 10,000 Men. II Psychosocial and Other Risk Factors as Evidenced by a Multi-Variate Analysis of a Five Year Incidence Study." *American Journal of Medicine*. Volume 60, Number 6, 1976, pages 910-921.

Medalie, J.H., K.C. Strange, S.J. Zyzanski and U. Goldbourt. "The Importance of Biopsychosocial Factors in the Development of Duodenal Ulcer in a Cohort of Middle-Aged Men." *Am J Epidemiol*. Volume 136, Number 10, 1992, pages 1280-1287.

Petro R. and A.D. Lopez. "WHO Consultative Group on Statistical Aspects of Tobacco-Related Mortality. Worldwide Mortality from Current Smoking Patterns." In *Tobacco and Health 1990: The Global War*. B. Durston and K. Jamrozik, Eds. Proceedings from the Seventh World Conference on Tobacco and Health, April 1-5, 1990, Perth, Western Australia.

Petro, R., A.D. Lopez, J. Boreham, M. Thun, and C. Heath. "Mortality from Tobacco in Developed Countries: Indirect Estimation from Vital Statistics." *Lancet*. Volume 339, 1992, pages 1268-1278.

Russek, L.G. and G.E. Schwartz. "Narrative Descriptions of Parental Love and Caring Predict Health Status in Midlife: A 35-year Follow-Up of the Harvard Mastery of Stress Study." *Altern Ther Health Med*. Volume 2, Number 6, November 1996, pages 55-62.

Schardt, David and Stephen Schmidt. "Caffeine: The Inside Scoop." *Nutrition Action Healthletter*. December 1996.

Seeman, T.C. and S.L. Syme. "Social Networks and Coronary Artery Disease: A Comparison of the Structure and Function of Social Relations as Predictors of Disease." *Psychosomatic Medicine*. Volume 49, Number 4, 1987, pages 341-354.

Spiegel, D. *Living Beyond Limits: New Hope and Help for Facing Life Threatening Illness*. New York, NY: Times Books, 1993.

Spiegel, D., J.R. Bloom, H.C. Draemer, and E. Gottheil. "Effect of Psychosocial Treatment on Survival of Patients with Metastatic Breast Cancer." *Lancet*. Volume 8668, Number 2, October 14, 1989, pages 888-891.

Steward, H.L., M.C. Bethea, S.S. Andrews and L.A. Balart. *Sugar Busters*. New York, NY: Ballantine Books, 1998.

Stryker, Jeff. "Hallelujah! Science Looks at Prayer for Friend and Fungus." New York *Times*. April 5, 1998.

Targ, Elizabeth. "Evaluating Distant Healing: A Research Review." *Alternative Therapies in Health and Medicine*. Volume 3, Number 6, November 1997, pages 74-78.

Wallis, Claudia. "Using Faith, Prayer and Spirituality to Improve Health: Press Review." *Time Australia*. June 24, 1996, Medicine section, page 86.

Webster's Dictionary. Ashland, OH: Landoll, Inc., 1993.

Whitmont, E.C. *The Alchemy of Healing*. California: North Atlantic Books, 1993.

Index

A

Abdomen 80
Abdominal irritation 28
Abductor, inner 80
Abnormal heart rates 114
Abstinence 71
Accidents 15, 42, 89
Accruciate ligament 43
Acid indigestion 114
ACL 43
Addicts 88, 91, 92, 109
Addiction 71, 87, 88, 91, 132
Adolescents 51, 54, 58, 61, 116, 126, 128
Adrenal glands 95
Aerobic capacity 69
Aerobic circuit exercise 61, 128
Aerobic dancing 50
Aerobic exercise 58, 59, 60, 65, 75, 125, 126, 127, 129, 130
AIDS 15, 65, 106
Alcohol 71, 109
Alcoholic 71, 126
Aloe vera 2, 16, 32, 36, 121, 124
Alternative health care provider 26
Alternative practitioner 26
Alternative treatments 25
Alzheimer's disease 32, 33
Ambrotose 32, 36
Angiography 116
Ankylosing spondylitis 94
Antibiotic 105

Antibodies 95, 96
Antihypertensive 59
Antioxidant 37, 69, 124, 126
Anxiety 62, 66, 70, 87, 130
Arms 80
Arthritic 68, 69
Arthritis 17, 65, 68, 69, 128, 129, 130
Athlete 27, 124, 126
Australia 54, 60, 66, 125, 133, 134
Autoimmune 130
Autoimmune disease 36

B

B vitamin 32, 33
Back 80, 86
Baked potato 111
Balance 57, 77, 130
Barbecue sauce 110
Bible 85, 115, 131, 132
Binge 127
Binge eaters 71
Birth defect 114
Bladder, cancer of 113
Blood glucose 61
Blood pressure 40, 106, 116, 125, 126, 127
Blood sugar level 111
Body fat 39, 56, 70
Bodybuilding 79

Bone density 45, 56, 57, 128
Bone loss 42, 55, 56, 123
Bone structure 57
Bread 111
Breast cancer 37, 56, 70, 118, 123, 124, 128, 130, 134
Breast lump 114
Broken bone 40
Bronchitis 113

C

Caffeine 112, 114, 115, 133
Calcium 32, 40, 42, 43, 44, 45, 122, 123, 124, 125
Calcium citrate 32, 39, 45, 122, 125
Calcium intake 42, 44, 124
Calves 80
Canadian 53, 54, 125
Canadian national obesity 54
Cancer 15, 35, 37, 55, 56, 65, 69, 70, 95, 107, 108, 113, 118, 119, 122, 123, 124, 125, 126, 127, 128, 129, 130, 134
Cancer cell 95
Candy bar 110
Carbo-loading 111
Cardiovascular disease 37, 57
Cardiovascular exercise 72, 78, 79
Cardiovascular fitness 60
Cardiovascular system 58, 59
CD4 95
CD4+ count 68
Centers for Disease Control 51, 52, 127, 133
Central nervous system 114
Cerebrovascular disease 60

Cheerful heart 85
Chemotherapy 108
Chest 74, 80, 127
Chest pain 116
Chocolate 112
Cholesterol 40, 59, 116, 127, 130
Cholesterol levels 59
Christian prayer 105
Chronic pain 65, 94
Chronic physical illness 65
Cigarette 14
Cigarette smoking 113
Cirrhosis 15
Citracal 32, 40, 45
Cleft palate 114
Colon cancer 37
Colorectal cancer 70, 125
Constipation 28
Consumer Reports on Health 67, 126
Corn 111
Coronary angiography 116
Coronary arteries 116
Coronary artery disease 60, 65, 127, 129, 133
Coronary blockage 116
Corticosteroid 95
Cortisol 63, 95, 123, 127
Cross country ski machine 75
Cross training 75

D

Daffodil bulb 20, 28
Death 15, 112, 113, 121, 133
Denial 88
Department of Agriculture 35, 125

Depression 36, 38, 62, 63, 64, 66, 111, 126, 127, 128, 129
Depressive symptoms 65, 71, 126
DHEA 2, 16, 33, 38, 121, 123, 124
Diabetes 61, 62, 111, 116, 125, 126, 128, 130
Diabetes, type I 61, 126
Diabetic 61, 62
Diaphragm 96
Diastolic blood pressure 58
Dietary supplements 27
Difficulty with relationships 88
Dioscorea villosa 33, 38
Disabilities 65, 126
Disease 2, 15, 16, 17, 21, 27, 28, 32, 33, 36, 37, 38, 49, 51, 52, 55, 57, 60, 65, 88, 94, 96, 97, 105, 111, 113, 117, 118, 122, 123, 127, 128, 129, 130, 133
Disease-fighting antibodies 96
Doctor 26, 30, 43, 55, 103, 104, 106, 120
Dopac 95
Drug addict 109

E

Eating disorder 71, 127
Elliptical walker 75
Emotional swing 29
Emotionally challenged 68
Emotionally charged 68
Emotionally supported 116
Emphysema 113
Enada 32, 33
Encouragement 6, 79, 119

Endorphin 65, 96
Energy 2, 16, 30, 60, 66, 76, 97, 115, 121
Energy level 30, 97
England 55
Enzyme 76, 77, 122, 126
ERT 44
Esophagus, cancer of 113
Estrogen 36, 37, 38, 44, 63, 122, 123, 124, 126
Exercise 2, 17, 18, 39, 47, 48, 49, 50, 51, 52, 53, 54, 55, 56, 57, 58, 59, 60, 61, 62, 64, 65, 66, 67, 68, 69, 70, 71, 72, 73, 74, 75, 77, 78, 79, 80, 82, 125, 126, 127, 128, 129, 130

F

Family history 32, 33, 37
Fatigue 51, 69, 70, 94, 111, 126, 128, 129
Female 37
Fever 105
Fiber 27, 124
Fibrous breast lumps 114
Firm 32, 38
Flower 14, 20, 28
Food 2, 16, 26, 29, 44, 71, 101, 102, 110, 111, 121, 123, 124, 125
Food addict 71
Forearms 80
Fracture 42, 43, 45, 55, 56, 126, 128, 129
Free radical 69
Fruit 35, 36

G

Gamma interferon 95
Gestational diabetes 62, 125
Gingko biloba 32, 33, 34, 122, 123, 125
Glucose level 61
Glucose load 110
Glucose overload 111
Glucose regulation 61
Glutes 80
Glycemic index 110, 111
Glyconutrient 2, 16, 32, 36, 38, 121, 124
Growth hormone 32, 39
Gym 19, 75, 78, 79, 115

H

Hamstring 80
HDL cholesterol 59
Headache 28, 29, 109, 114, 115
Healing 92, 93, 94, 98, 104, 105, 106, 107, 116
Healing prayer 106
Health care cost 15, 16, 27
Health expenditure 16
Heart disease 15, 38, 65, 130
Heart monitor 72, 73, 74
Herbal extract 45
Hernia 132
Hernia surgery 105
High blood pressure 116
High level wellness 1, 20, 21, 46, 48, 49, 55, 84, 98, 121
Hip fracture 56, 126, 129
HIV 15
Holistic health 26
Hormone replacement 37, 123
Hot flash 29, 38
Hyperactivity 111
Hypertension 114, 126, 132
Hysterectomy 37, 40, 107

I

Ice cream 110
Identity issue 88
Immune function 68
Immune system 36, 40, 95
Immunosuppressive 95
Impatience 88
Inactive 96
Inactivity 52
Infertility 114
Inflammation 68
Influenza 15
Insomnia 114
Insulin sensitivity 61
Insulin-dependent diabetes 61, 128
Intercellular communication 36
Internal jogging 96
Intimacy 115, 116
Irritability 88
Isoflavone 37, 122, 123, 124

J

Joint mobility 69
Joke 94
Joy 9, 87, 92, 94

K

Ketchup 110
Kidney stone 45

L

Larynx 113
Lateral collateral 43
Laughter 8, 84, 92, 93, 94, 95, 96, 97, 98, 131, 132
Laughter therapy 94
Laying on of hands 104, 105
LDL cholesterol 59
Lecithin 36
Leg 5, 6, 41, 43, 80
LifeSpan I 32, 39
Lipogenic enzyme 76, 77
Lipolytic enzyme 76, 77
Lipoprotein 130
Liver cancer 69, 126
Liver disease 15
Locus of control, internal 71
Long-term health 118
Longevity 96
Love 17, 18, 19, 22, 25, 29, 43, 66, 67, 73, 78, 86, 87, 89, 97, 98, 108, 109, 115, 116, 117, 118, 119, 120, 133
Loving 10, 99, 115, 118, 120, 132
Lung, cancer of 69, 113, 126
Lung disease 94

M

Macaroni 112
Macaroni and cheese 112
Major muscle groups 80
Malaise 66
Man-Aloe 32, 36, 42
Medical school 107
Meditation 102
Memory loss 33
Men 8, 38, 43, 44, 51, 54, 55, 59, 63, 70, 75, 76, 96, 116, 117, 133
Menopausal symptoms 29
Menopause 37
Mental health 64, 65, 66, 127
Mental health services 64
Mental processing 34
Metastatic breast cancer 118, 134
Migraine headache 28
Miracle 2, 16, 28, 36, 121, 124
Miscarriage 114
Monosaccharide 32, 36
Morphine 65
MRI 43
Muscle 45, 57, 58, 60, 69, 77, 79, 80, 96, 97
Muscle strength 69
Muscle tension 96

N

NADH 32, 33, 122
National Institute on Aging 55
National Institutes of Health 44, 124
National Nutrition Survey 54
Natural estrogen 36
Natural killer cell activity 91, 131
Natural painkiller 96
Natural therapies 25
Nausea 28, 70
Neurotransmitter 63
New England Journal of Medicine 26, 122
Nicotinamide adenine dinucleotide 33, 122

Night sweats 29
Non-insulin dependent 61
Nondrinker 27
Nurse 26, 42, 131
Nutraceutical 29, 30
Nutritional intake 101, 102
Nutritional supplementation 23, 26, 27, 28
Nutritional supplements 23, 26, 28, 29, 122
Nutritious eating 17

O

Obesity 53, 54, 111
Obstructive pulmonary disease 15
Oncological care 118
Oncologist 118
Oncology 106
Optimal health 46
Oral cavity 113
Osteoporosis 55, 37, 38, 42, 55, 56, 114, 123, 125, 129
Osteoporotic 56, 128
Outer abductors 80
Ovarian cancer 35, 56, 107, 118, 119
Overweight 52, 53, 54, 125

P

Pain 28, 41, 65, 69, 78, 94, 96, 105, 116
Painkiller 96
Pancreas 113
Panic attack 114
Parental love 117, 118, 133
Pasta 111

Perfectionism 88
Pharmaceutical 29
Pharmaceutical industry 28
Pharmacy student 27, 124
Pharynx 113
Physical disabilities 65, 126
Physical education 51, 58
Physical exercise 66, 129
Physical exertion 45
Physician 2, 9, 26, 29, 33, 62, 68, 106, 126
Phyt-Aloe 34, 35
Phyto-Bears 32, 34
Phytochemical 2, 16, 32, 35, 121, 123
Phytoestrogen 37, 38, 122, 123, 124
Plus 32, 33
PMS 38
Pneumonia 15, 105
Polymannan 2, 16, 121, 124
Poor communication 88
Postmenopausal 44, 45
Potatoes 111
Pray 104, 105, 106, 107
Prayer 100, 102, 103, 104, 105, 106, 107, 108, 119, 132, 134
Precursor 33, 38
Pregnancy 62
Pregnenolone 33, 38
Premature death 113
Prescribed drug 55
Preventive 17, 33, 37, 56, 61, 62, 69, 70, 123, 124
Primary care physician 26
Processed food 110
Profile 32, 39
Progressive involvement 88
Prostate cancer 37, 70, 124, 129

Protein 32, 36, 37
Protein drink mix 32, 36
Psychological well-being 70

Q

Quality of life 27, 28, 71, 125

R

Radiation therapy 70, 128
Radical hysterectomy 107
Recreation 83, 85, 86, 87, 128, 131
Reducing stress 67
Relationships 117
Relaxation technique 67
Resistance training 61, 75, 126
Respiration 96
Respiratory infection 113
Restlessness 66
Rheumatoid arthritis 68, 128, 129, 130
Rice 111
Rigid thinking 88
Rollerblade 75
Run 75, 81, 91, 111
Running 6, 8, 41, 43, 50, 51, 69, 81, 86, 126

S

Salad dressing 110
Scientific studies 104
Scotland 55
Sedentary 57, 67, 68, 69
Self-esteem 66, 67, 70, 127, 130
Self-neglect 88
Serotonin 63
Shaklee Energizing Soy 32

Sharpening focus 34
Shoulders 80
Side effects 28, 29
Skiing trainer 75
Slapstick movie 94
Smoking 112, 113, 114, 133
Social stigma 63
Social support 117
Soy lecithin 36
Soy protein 32, 36, 37
Soymilk 112
Spine 45, 94
Sport 32, 45, 55, 124, 126, 127, 128, 129, 130
Sports Council and Health Education Council survey 55
Stabilized *Aloe vera* 32, 36
Stair stepper 75
Stationary bike 75
Stationary bike riding 59
Stimulant 114
Stomach ulcers 113, 117
Stress 67, 92, 93, 95, 97, 131, 132, 133
Stress hormone 95, 131
Stress reaction 62
Stress-related illness 97
Stressed out 67
Stroke 15, 89
Sugar 108, 109, 110, 111, 112, 134
Sugar-free 112
Suicide 15
Supplement 23, 24, 26, 27, 28, 29, 30, 31, 32, 34, 36, 39, 43, 44, 45, 46, 122, 123, 124, 125
Support group 89, 118, 119

Surgeon General 51, 113, 127, 130
Switzerland 54

T

T cells 95
T-helper cell count 95
Tai chi 66, 127
Target heart range 73, 74
Tension 66, 67, 93, 96, 114, 126, 132
Therapy 26, 37, 43, 44, 66, 70, 71, 94, 108, 123, 125, 126, 128
Thigh cream 38
Tibia plateau fracture 42, 43
Tobacco 113, 132, 133
Tofu cheese 112
Transdermal application 38
Transdermal form 32
Treadmill 75
Triceps 80

U

Ulcers 113, 114, 117
Unconventional therapy 26
United States Department of Agriculture 35, 125
Uterine cancer 56

V

Vegetable 35
Vitamin supplement 32, 39

W

Walk 6, 53, 64, 66, 67, 68, 69, 115
Walking 43, 52, 54, 64, 67, 127
Weight lifting 78
Weight loss 54, 101
Weight training 126
Weight training program 78
Wellness 1, 7, 16, 18, 20, 21, 22, 28, 46, 48, 49, 55, 84, 98, 102, 121
White bread 111
White pasta 111
White rice 111
Whole-wheat macaroni 112
Wild Mexican yam 32, 38, 45
Withdrawal 88, 115
Women 6, 27, 37, 44, 45, 51, 54, 55, 56, 57, 59, 60, 62, 63, 70, 75, 76, 77, 96, 108, 118, 123, 126, 127, 128, 129, 130
Women runners 59
Work addiction 87, 88, 91, 92, 132
Work binge 88
Wound healing 105

Z

Zestful living 21, 22

Also by Dr. Neecie Moore

✻ *The Missing Link:*
   The Facts about Glyconutrients

✻ *Designing Your Life with Designer Foods:*
   The Facts about Phytochemicals

✻ *The Miracle in Aloe Vera:*
   The Facts about Polymannans

✻ *Bountiful Health, Boundless Energy, Brilliant Youth:*
   The Facts about DHEA

The Missing Link is $14.95 plus s&h
All others, $12.95 each plus s&h

To order, phone toll-free,

1-888-499-9888.

Validation press
10002 Aurora N, Ste 3313
Seattle, WA 98133-9347

Telephone: (206)782-3111
Facsimile: (206)789-6495
E-mail: Validman@aol.com